WOMEN OPENIN

IMMEASURABLY MORE

CASANDRA MARTIN

A 21st Century Christian Publication

ISBN-13: 978-0-89098-303-4

Cover design by Jonathan Edelhuber

Back cover illustration by Caleb Gray

Immeasurably More

"Now to him who is able to do immeasurably more than all we ask or imagine,
according to his power that is at work within us,
to him be glory in the church and in Christ Jesus throughout all generations,
for ever and ever! Amen." – Ephesians 3:20-21, NIV 1984

You are God's delight and His great desire. He has a dream for you that begins today and stretches into eternity. It is a plan for you to live so abundantly, so fully, so deeply in Him that your life overflows with His Immeasurably More. Immeasurably More is a boundary marker. It describes the extent to which God will go to bring you home, the limits of His love for you, the amount of power He is able to pour into your life, and the grace with which He is willing to fill you. Immeasurably More is also a picture of the life He wants you to live in Him – how far He wants you to stretch, how big He longs for you to dream, and how deep He desires for you to travel into His heart.

Too often we settle for less that God's Immeasurably More. The Book of Ephesians challenges us to set our sights higher, walk more confidently, pray more fervently, and kneel more humbly before a God whose greatest delight is give us Immeasurably More of Himself.

Welcome to WOW!

Women Opening the Word is a Bible study series designed to help women more richly and fully experience the presence of God. Meeting God in the pages of a WOW study opens your eyes to the wonder of God's love and the purpose of living deeply in His presence. Transformation is at the heart of studying the Bible. God wants you to be transformed into His likeness – to look like Jesus. The WOW Bible studies help you to answer the call to live as changed women – cross-shaped, resurrection-empowered, faith-driven, Christ-exalting women.

Whether you use the study in a classroom or small group setting, or in your personal quiet time, WOW focuses on answering three challenges every woman who longs to live closer to God faces: ***Commitment*** – WOW's four-day format is designed to help you find the time and develop the discipline of daily Bible study. ***Confidence*** – At times, Bible study seems intimidating and overwhelming. WOW guides you on a walk through Scripture to seek God's face and experience His transformation as you connect God's truth directly with your life. ***Creativity*** – When studying the Bible feels stale, the WOW studies provide refreshing and innovative ways to encounter God through a variety of study methods, insights, and the following special features:

Day 1 Each lesson is broken into four parts. As you begin a lesson, start with Day 1. Work
- through the first day – open your Bible, enjoy the time with God, and experience the
Day 4 life-changing lessons He has planned for you. Tomorrow study Day 2, and so forth. The WOW studies are designed this way in order help you spend daily time deep in the presence of God. There are many lessons, treasures, and blessings God wants to pour into you as you spend time with Him in His Word. Spreading out each lesson over four days provides the best opportunity for you to absorb as much richness as you can from your time with God.

Open Your Bible! – When you see this symbol, it indicates an opportunity to open your Bible and meet God in its pages. God speaks to you through His Word. He longs for you to take off your sandals and draw near to Him on holy ground. Choose an accurate, reliable, and readable translation. This study specifically refers to the ESV – English Standard Version. You are welcome to use any translation that you prefer. The important thing is to open your Bible and prepare your heart to meet your amazing God.

Compass Question – The Compass symbol invites you to slow down and answer a question that speaks directly to your heart, pointing it to the truths that move you toward transformation. They are thought questions. Everyone's answers will be personal and unique. They are designed to help God's Word speak directly to your life.

To the Heart – These are messages from my heart to yours. These special thoughts have one purpose – to help you experience the glorious richness of God's love in a very personal and intimate way.

Choose a Home For Your Heart – Living in God's Immeasurably More always begins with a choice. Where will I live? What path will I walk? At the end of Days 2 and 4, there are places for you to stop and do a location check. The location check is designed to help you examine your heart in the light of the lessons God reveals through our walk through Ephesians. ***It'll Do Lane*** helps define the ways the world encourages you to settle for less than God's best. ***Immeasurably More*** focuses your attention on what it means to live within the abundant blessings of His presence. ***Choose a Home For Your Heart*** is the location test. Here you will find a question or activity meant to help you look deeply at your own heart in the light of God's grace and His desire for you. Your answers will help reveal where God wants to work in your life, places that require surrender, and obstacles that are keeping you from living the Immeasurably More life Jesus wants to give you.

Leading a WOW Study

Leading a WOW study is primarily about opening the door to the presence of God and helping the people you are with make the journey. You already have the tools you need – a willing and loving heart, prayer, your Bible, the help of the Holy Spirit, and your WOW book.

There are as many different ways to effectively use a WOW study as there are people excited about meeting God in His Word. The WOW studies are designed to be flexible and allow you to adapt the study to your individual and group needs. Be creative! The WOW studies are tools meant to help you dig deeply into God's Word. Use them in the way that best helps you meet God, experience the depth of His love, and be transformed into the likeness of His Son.

If you are leading a WOW study in a **45-minute Bible class format** –

Commit to spending time in prayer and study. Pray for the women in your group. Ask God to create an environment among your women that will allow Him full access to every heart. As you study, remember to honor the truth that you are meeting God in the pages of His Word. Let His love touch you first; then prepare to share that love with others. Leaders always receive deep blessings from the time spent preparing to share God's Word with others.

Divide each lesson into two parts. Using the Day 1-4 markers, ask your class to study Days 1 and 2 on week one, Days 3 and 4 on week two, and so forth. There is enough material in each two-day block to meet the needs of your class time.

Use the Choose a Home For Your Heart chart at the end of Days 2 and 4 to help you focus on the main points of the lesson. This is the one truth that you want the class to walk away with at the end of your time together. Use them to guide your preparation and the direction of the class.

Allow the class to be discussion-oriented. The Compass Questions are designed to open the door for sharing thoughts, feelings, questions, and perspectives. It often takes time for women to open their hearts and be transparent. Be patient and loving. This time of discussion will help each woman plant the truth of God's Word deeply into their heart.

Keep your eyes open for the ways God is working among you. Take special note of the many ways God is blessing your time together as a group of women studying His Word. Let that awareness be a springboard for praise, thanksgiving, and renewed surrender.

If you are leading a WOW study in a **90-minute women's Bible study format** –

Commit to spending time in prayer and study. Pray for the women in your group. Ask God to create an environment among your women that will allow Him full access to every heart. As you study, remember to honor the truth that you are meeting God in the pages of His Word. Let His love touch you first; then prepare to share that love with others. Leaders always receive deep blessings from the time spent preparing to share God's Word with others.

Do one lesson per week or divide the lesson into two pieces. – This depends on your schedule and the amount of time your women want to devote to the study. Either way – there will be enough material to meet your needs.

Use the Choose a Home For Your Heart chart at the end of Days 2 and 4 to help you focus on the main points of the lesson. These are the truths that you want the class to walk away with at the end of your time together. Use them to guide your preparation and the direction of the class.

Allow the class to be discussion-oriented. The Compass Questions are designed to open the door for sharing thoughts, feelings, questions, and perspectives. It often takes time for women to open their hearts and be transparent. Be patient and loving. This time of discussion will help each woman plant the truth of God's Word deeply into their heart.

Keep your eyes open for the ways God is working among you. Take special note of the many ways God is blessing your time together as a group of women studying His Word. Let that awareness be a springboard for praise, thanksgiving, and renewed surrender.

If you are using a WOW study for **personal study**–

Commit to spending time in prayer as you study. Prayer is indispensible to preparing your heart to meet God. Prayer and study go hand-in-hand and allow your heart to respond to the truths and direction God is teaching you.

Use the Day markers to help guide you in daily Bible study. As you begin a lesson, begin with Day 1. Work through the first day – open your Bible, enjoy the time with God, and experience the life-changing lessons He has planned for you. Tomorrow study Day 2, and so forth. The WOW study is designed this way in order help you spend daily time deep in the presence of God.

Use the Choose a Home For Your Heart chart at the end of Days 2 and 4. Open your heart to the deep transformation God wants to work in your life.

Keep your eyes open for the ways God is working in you. Take special note of the many ways God is blessing your time with Him. Let that awareness be a springboard for praise, thanksgiving, and renewed surrender.

Joy for the Journey

May God richly bless you as you spend this time in His Word. He has so many treasures to share with you because you are the treasure of His heart. Know that as you study, you are covered with prayer and thanksgiving. My prayer is that you will be able to see God's words fully take shape in your life as you commit your heart to living in His Immeasurably More.

Casandra

Table of Contents

Introduction i

Lesson 1 — It'll Do 1

Lesson 2 — Immeasurably More 15

Lesson 3 — Immeasurable Love 29

Lesson 4 — Immeasurable Power 43

Lesson 5 — Immeasurable Grace 57

Lesson 6 — Immeasurable Peace 71

Lesson 7 — Immeasurable Purpose 85

Lesson 8 — Immeasurable Faith 99

Lesson 9 — Walk Called 113

Lesson 10 — Walk Changed 127

Lesson 11 — Walk Closely 141

Lesson 12 — Walk Committed 155

Lesson 13 — Walk Confidently 169

Bibliography 183

It'll Do
Lesson 1

Welcome to WOW! We have such an exciting journey ahead of us. God has more in mind for you than you can possibly imagine for yourself. He longs to meet you in the pages of His Word. He is passionate about showing you His heart. He yearns for you to throw open the door of your soul and allow Him full access to every part of who you are. As you begin today, pray for open eyes to see the Immeasurably More He has in store for you. Pray for courage to walk in the bigger life He has planned for you. Pray for your heart to be ready to embrace the joy you are about to encounter, the peace you are about to experience, and the fullness you are about to enjoy.

Day 1

I was driving through central Texas. It was a hot summer day. All of the kids I was driving back from a VBS mission trip were asleep in the back of the van. That is when I saw the small street that intersected the road on which I was traveling. I glanced at the street sign, and started to laugh. The name of the road was It'll Do Lane.

I imagined the path that led someone to name the place where they live "It'll Do Lane." Tired and weary, they looked around, said, "It'll do" and decided to stop. This was good enough, far enough, and satisfying enough to make a place to plant a family and spend a lifetime. They built a life on It'll Do Lane. They raised their children in the shadow of its sign. They defined their dreams, stretched their imagination, and decided to be satisfied with It'll Do.

Too many of us live on It'll Do Lane.

Immeasurably More

We tend to settle for "good enough" lives. We make It'll Do the residence of our hearts, hopes, and dreams. As long as there is a little more happiness than sorrow, pleasure than pain, blessings than burdens, and satisfaction than sacrifice, we consider ourselves as coming out ahead in the game of life.

But God never meant for us to live "good enough" lives. He doesn't want It'll Do Lane to be the address of our hearts. Deep down inside, we know it. Our souls were never meant to settle for It'll Do. The good enough life feels a little empty, and at the strangest moments we catch ourselves longing for more.

Why do you think we settle for It'll Do?

God has a different address in mind for you. How does Abundance Avenue sound? Wouldn't you rather live on Blessing Boulevard or Wonderful Way? He wants you to take up residence at the intersection of Immeasurably More and Infinite Possibilities.

His plan has always been for us to experience abundant, rich, overflowing lives. Lives filled with wonder, joy, confidence, and peace.

This is the Immeasurably More God has in mind for you. Lives so defined by His presence, so immersed in His power, and so soaked in His grace that we draw the eyes of those around us to the cross.

Write Ephesians 3:20.

Here is a promise that speaks to the deep longings of our hearts. Deep down, we know that we are not meant to settle for It'll Do. *Good enough* are words that our hearts accept because the possibility of anything more seems impossible, scary, or too painful to dream about any longer.

The words embedded in the Ephesian letter contain the assurance that Immeasurably More is not only possible, but meant just for us.

"Now to him who is able..." (NIV) Here is the key to the Immeasurably More life. God is able. Our faith has to find its footing in the deep truth that He is able. He is able to love us like He tells us He does. He is able to forgive us with the grace He promises us. He is able to keep His word, honor His holiness, and offer transformation to hearts that desperately need His touch.

Why is it so important that we understand that God is able?

If God is able, then the door of possibility is thrown wide open. Understanding that God is able is the foundation on which our faith must rest. We must believe that He is powerful enough, faithful enough, wise enough, good enough, holy enough, loving enough, and enduring enough to accomplish all that He has set before us. Many of our doubts, reservations, and questions find their roots in the way that we limit or put boundaries on the truth that God is able.

"to do immeasurably more than all we ask or imagine,..." (NIV) When we embrace the reality that God is able, it pushes back the boundaries of what is possible. My boundaries are not set by the limits of my own strength, wisdom, or resources. They are set in the infinite goodness and matchless love of God. What I ask for is just the starting line. What I can imagine is just the beginning of the yard stick, the zero on the scale, and the driveway from which we begin our journey. Too often, we settle for flying paper planes while God intends for us to travel with Him into the stars.

Look up the word *immeasurably* in the dictionary. How does that definition help you understand the life God has in mind for you?

"according to his power that is at work within us." (NIV) This is the most exciting news of all. His power is at work in you. Here is the fuel that drives the Immeasurably More life He wants to give us. Here is the strength that will break through the obstacles, tear down the fences, and remove the barriers that keep us on It'll Do Lane. His power is moving, transforming, creating, implementing, and building His dream within your heart. It might seem strange to think that God is at work within you as you do the dishes, go to work, answer the phone, or read your email, but He is. He uses every moment, every opportunity, and every situation to offer you the Immeasurably More life.

Read Romans 8:28. How does this passage outline the way God's power is at work in you?

Day 2

Ephesians is our guidebook into the Immeasurably More life. In its pages, we will be able to capture a picture of the Immeasurably More God is offering us, see the good enough for which we often settle, and discover the pathway to leaving It'll Do behind and embracing the rich abundance for which we were made.

As we approach the Book of Ephesians, we need to stop and look at some barriers that tend to get in the way of embracing the Immeasurably More life. Barriers can be anything that prevents our movement into the will and purpose of God. The barriers that keep us on It'll Do Lane tend to be set in our minds rather than our circumstances. Changing how we see can go a long way to changing how far we can go.

What questions or barriers do you think might be keeping you from living the Immeasurably More life?

Barrier #1 – I don't know what the Immeasurably More life looks like.

It is hard to know where you are going if you don't have a destination in mind. We end up traveling in circles, feeling like we are wandering aimlessly through our days. Any motion seems better than no movement at all, so we keep taking one more step in the hope that it is leading us in the right direction.

God wants you to walk with purpose. His will for you lays out a map that leads directly into the Immeasurably More life. The world holds up a lot of pictures of what a full, abundant, satisfying life should look like – lots of money, glamorous beauty, big houses filled with expensive things, a powerful job, influential friends, days filled with travel to exotic places, and a carefree, all-about-me attitude. We are bombarded with images of the life the world wants us to strive after and we let those images define our peace, shape our contentment, direct our choices, and order our priorities. But God has something so much better in mind for you.

The Immeasurably More life is not about the things you have, the people you know, the job you hold, or the balance of your bank account. You can live the Immeasurably More life in a one bedroom apartment, a big house, a tent by the creek, or a high rise building. You can be everything God calls you to be working as a clerk at the grocery store, a teacher, an executive, a nurse, a stay-at-home mom, a secretary, a homemaker, or a captain of industry.

The Immeasurably More life is not about the stuff you have, but about the stuff of which you are made. It is about the stuff we put into our hearts, the stuff with which we fill our minds, and the stuff we allow to define our souls.

God's power is at work in you with a very specific purpose – to change your stuff. He wants to throw out the guilty, shame-laden, sin-encrusted stuff and fill you with Jesus. That transformation is at the heart of the Immeasurably More life.

How is Jesus the best picture of God's Immeasurably More?

Barrier #2 – I don't know if God's Immeasurably More is for me.

Okay, God has an Immeasurably More plan for His people. It probably works great for those super-saints who have it all together, but not people like me. I struggle with sin, wrestle with doubt, and walk far too often in my own desires. I don't know enough about the Bible. My prayers feel a little stale, and I am not nearly as talented as the woman who sits three pews over. Honestly, I am just not good enough, holy enough, wise enough, or spiritual enough to change where I live. Besides, I am barely hanging on where I am at. If I can't get it together on It'll Do Lane, how will I ever be able to live in God's Immeasurably More?

Jesus came to crucify the myth that you weren't meant for the Immeasurably More life. God couldn't imagine an eternity without you, so He stepped out of glory into a world of darkness in order to bring you home. He loves you with an intensity that will take your breath away. His power is at work within you in order to shatter the It'll Do barriers that keep you from living within His Immeasurably More.

Read Matthew 17:20-21. What is the key to living a life beyond what you can ask or imagine?

Immeasurably More

The key word here is *faith*. Faith provides the glasses that let you imagine that the Immeasurably More life can be yours. Faith invests itself in the truth that God is able and willing to work in the lives of people He loves. Even people who struggle with sin. Even people who are barely getting by. Even people with faith as small as the tiniest seed. Even people like me.

Barrier #3 – I don't know how to get from where I am to God's Immeasurably More.

It all sounds great, but I don't even know where to begin. Some days, mustard seed faith seems like a stretch for me. How will I know if I am traveling in the right direction?

Write John 14:6.

Here is the great news about the Immeasurably More life. It is all wrapped up in Jesus. He is the Way. When we walk with Him and in His will, we will find ourselves living in His Immeasurably More. His Word is the lamp that lights our way. His love dispels the fogs of doubt and despair that darken our days. His power fuels the transformation that is necessary for us to experience the Immeasurably More He has in mind for us.

Read Jeremiah 29:11. What kind of plans does God have for you?

Make a list of five words that describe life on It'll Do Lane.

Make a list of five words that describe the Immeasurably More life God wants for you.

It'll Do or Immeasurably More? It is your choice. Use this time to talk to God about where your heart most wants to live.

Day 3

Our road map into the Immeasurably More life is found in the pages of the letter written by the apostle Paul to the Christians in Ephesus. Known to us as Ephesians, this book of the Bible was penned while Paul was in Rome, chained to a Roman soldier while awaiting trial before Caesar in approximately 60-62 A.D.

Paul wrote to the Christians he loved from his travels in Asia, especially his three-year stay in the capital city of Ephesus. We first meet the Christians in Ephesus in the pages of Acts. It is here in Acts 19 that we get a glimpse into Paul's time with the people to whom Ephesians is written. In getting to know them, we meet ourselves. As Paul walks toward Ephesus, we learn how to take the first steps into the Immeasurably More life.

Read Acts 19:1-7.

Who does Paul meet as he travels the inland path toward Ephesus?

deciples

What does Paul ask them? What is their response?

Did they receive the Holy Spirit - They were baptized by JOHN

To whom does the teaching of John point?

Jesus

What do these twelve men do after hearing about Jesus?

Baptized

Paul's third missionary journey is based entirely in the city of Ephesus. Traveling inland through the mountainous region from Phyrgia into Asia, Paul walks on a highway that leads through the interior country toward Ephesus, which is built on some hills by the sea.[1]

On his journey, Paul meets a company of twelve men, disciples of John the Baptizer. John's ministry focused on preparing the hearts of those who would commit to waiting for the coming of Jesus.

Immeasurably More

Read Luke 3:15-17. What is the thrust of John's message?

He was getting everyone prepared.

Having been baptized into John's baptism of repentance and preparation, these disciples now live a life of anticipation. They wait expectantly for the Immeasurably More the Messiah will one day bring.

Paul shares good news with John's disciples. The Immeasurably More life they long for is available today. No more waiting. Jesus is the fullness of everything God wants to do in their lives. The journey into Immeasurably More begins with full surrender to the person and purpose of Jesus. The men are baptized into the name of the Lord Jesus. Because they don't have the assurances of the written Scriptures, God allows them the mercy of an outward manifestation of the Spirit so they can be sure that the presence of God now dwells within them.

In this amazing picture, we catch our first road marker into the Immeasurably More life. The first "more" that God wants to give us is Himself. He wants to live within us, dwell within our hearts, guide our minds, direct our bodies, and make His home in our souls. He wants to fill us with His Spirit. He longs for the character of Jesus to take shape in our lives. He wants to move in and flood our lives with His light, grace, love, peace, compassion, mercy, and joy.

Immeasurably More finds its best definition in learning to live fully and completely in the presence of God.

Surrender and obedience are the tools we are given to take the first steps into God's Immeasurably More. We can't live in God's Immeasurably More if we are full of ourselves. In order to be full of God, we must empty ourselves of self, dying to the person who lives on It'll Do Lane. The waters of baptism become the graveyard where we leave the old person behind and come into contact with the life-changing, grace-bestowing, fear-erasing, love-enhancing, sin-destroying blood of Jesus.

Read Romans 6:3-4. Describe how the new life in which we now walk because of Jesus opens the door to living the Immeasurably More life.

We have a New life. We fill ourselves with Gods Spirit.

When we are baptized into the name of the Lord Jesus, we receive the gift of the Holy Spirit. God moves in and fills us with Himself. This is where Immeasurably More begins – with the presence of God in our lives. All of the good things we long for find their fulfillment in His Spirit. All of the questions we ask find their best answer in Jesus. All of the hopes and dreams that fill our souls find their outlet in the presence of God in our lives.

The process that begins at baptism grows and expands every day after we rise from the water. Each day we make the choice whether or not to allow God full access to our lives. Do we want to be full of self or full of Him? Every time I give more of myself to Him, His Spirit moves in deeper and reshapes me a little bit more for His glory. Each moment that finds me holding onto the pieces of my It'll Do life pushes the dreams God has for me a little further away.

The disciples on the road to Ephesus could have settled for It'll Do. They could have decided that what John had taught them was enough, and that they would stay where they were. Instead, they made a choice for Immeasurably More. They surrendered to the name of Jesus, and God filled them with the very best "more" He could give them – Himself.

How does their story encourage you to surrender to Jesus today?

Day 4

Paul arrives in Ephesus having given us the key to living the Immeasurably More life. The antidote to living on It'll Do Lane is found in Jesus. The "more" we long for is best satisfied in the presence of God. He fills us with Himself, and invites us into the adventure of living our lives soaked in all of the fullness, abundance, satisfaction, and blessing that comes from dwelling deeply in Him.

Approaching Ephesus, we find a city that has a familiar rhythm. Ephesus is a powerful, wealthy, influential center of power. It lies on the trade routes that connect Asia to the rest of the world. It plays host to travelers, merchants, and seekers from every land, language, and religion. It has a thriving economy, and one of the greatest markets in the Roman Empire. It boasts one of the seven wonders of the ancient world in its temple to the Greek goddess Artemis. Ephesus stands at the crossroads as one of the most defining cities in the Empire, and lives as a melting pot of beliefs and ideas from all over the world.

Read Acts 19:8-20.

Describe how Paul speaks among the people in the synagogue.

Describe the power God displays through Paul in Ephesus.

Immeasurably More

What happens to the seven sons of Sceva?

What do the believers burn in the sight of all the people?

What is the impact of the way God moves among the people of Ephesus?

Paul moves into Ephesus and begins to teach about Jesus. He boldly speaks the name of the Lord, reasoning and persuading with the people who listen about the kingdom of God. It is within the lessons that Paul teaches here that we catch our next glimpse of Immeasurably More. The kingdom of God is the address of a heart that seeks His Immeasurably More. Moving away from It'll Do Lane, citizens of the kingdom take up residence in the shadow of God's sovereignty. The kingdom defines the boundaries of God's rule. It is where His promises are lived out, His blessings are enjoyed, His provision is most clearly seen, and His purpose is embraced.

How does the world encourage us to be kings of our own lives?

How will surrendering the throne of our hearts to God open the door to the Immeasurably More life?

While ever calling and entreating, God will not inhabit space where He is not welcomed. Paul leaves the synagogue and takes up residence in the lecture hall of Tyrannus. From this platform, the entire region of Asia hears the word of the Lord.

In addition to the proclamation of God's Word, Paul is empowered by the Spirit to perform miraculous signs that confirm the truthfulness of his message. The sick are healed of their diseases, and those held prisoner by evil spirits are set free.

The power displayed by Paul captures the attention of the sons of Sceva who attempt to use the name of Jesus for their own glory and position. In a moment that opens our eyes to the spiritual battle around us, the demons declare that they know the name of Jesus and even His servant Paul, but they refuse to bow to the authority of pretenders who misuse His name. Naked and wounded, the sons of Sceva flee from the house. Their lack of respect inspires others in the city to hold the name of Jesus in reverence.

Here we find another truth about the Immeasurably More life. It can't be lived in compromise. *Compromise* sounds like such a reasonable word. Find middle ground. Give a little, take a little. Look for a happy medium. Don't put all your eggs in one basket. Compromise allows us to hedge our bets, hold back a little of our hearts, and maintain some control while looking like we are moving in the right direction.

The problem is that there is no room for compromise when it comes to faith. Jesus wants it all. No holding back, no leaving room to maneuver, no hanging on to bits and pieces. He demands full surrender, complete obedience, and absolute devotion. Not because He is a dictator with an authority complex, but because He knows that it is the only way into the Immeasurably More life we were made to live.

Look up *compromise* in the dictionary. How does its definition help you see its connection to living on It'll Do Lane?

The Ephesian Christians show us how to release the compromise that threatens our journey into God's Immeasurably More. Examining their lives and what was hidden in their hearts, they moved from compromise to commitment. Their actions reveal three necessary steps that set our feet on the path out of It'll Do Lane and point our hearts toward Immeasurably More.

"Also many of those who were now believers came, confessing and divulging their practices." Here is a beautiful picture – Christians coming together and opening their hearts. They talk about their struggles. They confess their weaknesses. They open up their lives, behavior, attitudes, and actions and put them on the table. They link arms and encourage each other. They hold one another to the standard of Jesus, committing together to living lives that celebrate and honor His holiness.

Immeasurably More

Accountability and transparency are essential if I want to live an Immeasurably More life. Left on my own, I have a tendency to rationalize my choices, dress up my bad decisions, and justify my motives and desires. Transparency allows others to see into my heart and help me walk in His way. Accountability is an act of surrender that acknowledges I can't do it on my own, and honors the truth that God sets me in a family in order to help me grow and become all He calls me to be.

Read James 5:16. With whom are you consistently transparent and accountable in confession and prayer? How do we develop these kinds of relationships?

"And a number of those who had practiced magic arts brought their books together and burned them in the sight of all." Here is a step into deep surrender and His Immeasurably More. The Christians in Ephesus do more than confess their compromise. They take action by burning the books that bind their hearts to It'll Do Lane. They don't pack them up and donate them. They don't put them in a closet. They burn them, cutting the ties that hold them back from embracing the fullness of God's Immeasurably More.

Read Luke 9:23. Take inventory. Is there anything you need to burn, deny, get rid of, or move out in order to rise above the compromise that keeps us on It'll Do Lane?

"And they counted the value of them and found it came to fifty thousand pieces of silver." This isn't just an interesting side note. They count the cost of compromise and commitment. Fifty thousand pieces of silver is an incredible amount of money. One piece of silver represents a day's wages. Fifty thousand pieces of silver equals 136 years' worth of wages. Too often, we sell our souls so cheaply and invest our hearts in trinkets rather than the priceless treasure of God's presence. They look at the value of the books that hold pieces of their hearts and the value of what God is offering them, and burn the books. They determine that God's Immeasurably More is infinitely more precious than any possession or amount of profit.

Read Luke 9:25. What kinds of things are people willing to trade for their souls? How do we learn to value commitment over compromise?

It'll Do Lane

Compromise is the name of the game. I can walk with Jesus while still holding on to a few things that really aren't that bad. Good enough is good enough.

Immeasurably More

Surrender and commitment are essential elements of the Immeasurably More life. God wants all of me so that He can fill every part of me with His abundance.

Choosing a Home For Your Heart

Pray for open eyes and a tender heart. Ask God to show you where you tend to compromise. Ask Him for the courage to leave good enough behind and walk in His Immeasurably More.

[1] Conybeare & Howson, p410-11

Immeasurably More Lesson 2

God calls us away from It'll Do Lane into His Immeasurably More. He longs for us to make His presence the address of our hearts. He wants you to experience all the contentment, peace, joy, and abundance that He has in mind for you. Sometimes we think that God's abundance will take shape in our lives when everything comes together and there are no more struggles. If we can just get through this problem, work out this difficulty, or conquer this sin, then perhaps we will be able to move from It'll Do into the more God promises. We put off living in God's Immeasurably More because we think that our lives have to be perfect in order for us to experience it. But this amazing more that He has planned for you is designed to be lived right now, exactly where you are.

Day 1

In Ephesus, we meet Christians who teach us that surrender and commitment are the first steps into the Immeasurably More life. The very first more that God wants to give us is Himself. He fills those who surrender their lives to Jesus with His Spirit. He moves in and begins the process of transforming us. As we learn to live in His presence, we see the compromises we tend to make with the world. There is baggage we have to let go of if we are going to move off of It'll Do Lane into His Immeasurably More.

Read Acts 19:20. What impact does the word of the Lord have in Ephesus?

Immeasurably More

How will God's Word impact our hearts as we shed the things that hold us to It'll Do Lane and embrace the Immeasurably More life?

We tend to read that verse as a generic description of what happens in Ephesus and Asia Minor. But God's Word always centers in the hearts of people. When we commit to walking in His will, His Word, with all of its power, light, grace, and wisdom increases and grows in our lives. It fills empty spaces and repairs the brokenness left by settling for good enough. The Word of the Lord begins to prevail mightily over the attitudes, behaviors, perspectives, and choices that once defined us, redirecting our energies, hopes, dreams, and expectations into the Immeasurably More He wants to shape within us.

Read Acts 19:23-41.

About what does there arise a great disturbance?

What charge does Demetrius bring against Paul?

What do the people do?

How does the town clerk finally quiet the crowd?

Paul spends three years in Ephesus preaching the good news of Jesus and calling people away from the good enough life into God's Immeasurably More. The impact in the region is powerful. All the residents of Asia hear the Word of the Lord and the life-changing message of the cross. So dramatic is the effect, so intense is the transformation that it rocks the economic and political structures in this city.

Known as the Way, the message of Jesus spreads from heart to heart as the map showing how to move from sin, selfishness, and self-reliance into a life defined by God's grace and goodness.

Read John 10:9, John 14:6, and Acts 4:12. Why is the Way a good description of the Christian life?

The city of Ephesus was renowned for its temple to the Greek goddess Artemis. The temple structure itself was considered one of the seven wonders of the ancient world. Artemis was a goddess of fertility and magic. Her image was said to have fallen from the sky, which the Ephesians believed marked them as chosen by the goddess to be her caretaker.

A great temple structure arose in Ephesus to honor Artemis. It was 425 feet long and 220 feet wide. Its open air structure was supported by 127 white marble columns, each 62 feet high and 6 feet in diameter.[1] Each column was a gift from a king in support of the goddess the temple honored.[2]

At the center of this immense temple was the image of Artemis herself. Pictured as a many-breasted woman, Artemis was an eclectic mix of Roman, Asian, Greek, and Egyptian mythology. Served by a combination of castrated priests, virgin priestesses, and temple prostitutes, Artemis held a powerful grip on the hearts of the people of Asia Minor.

Her temple became a repository for vast sums of money dedicated to the upkeep and support of the goddess. As a result, the temple of Artemis served as a key banking center for the region, tying the worship of Artemis not only to the religious life of Ephesus, but serving as a major component in the economic and political stability of the area.

What kinds of idols hold Artemis-like status in our society?

How does the way that the worship of Artemis wound its way into every aspect of Ephesian life help us to see the power the world has to hold us on It'll Do Lane?

Day 2

In Ephesus, the strangle hold of It'll Do Lane comes into direct conflict with the Immeasurably More way of Jesus.

After three years, there is dramatic evidence of the power of God's grace throughout the region of Asia Minor. Demetrius rises to speak for the trade guild of craftsmen who make silver shrines for visitors to Artemis' temple to take home with them. It is in his complaint about Paul that we see the powerful impact the cross has on those who commit their lives to Jesus.

Read Acts 19:23-27. What impact has the message of Jesus made in Ephesus?

Demetrius gathers his fellow tradesmen together to discuss the increasingly damaging impact Paul and his message are having on the sale of Artemis merchandise. The changed lives of the followers of the Way are having a marked effect on the ability of the craftsmen in the city to make a living. People who surrender to Jesus no longer come to the temple to worship, sacrifice, buy trinkets, or invest in exploring the deep mysteries of Artemis. Not only is their livelihood threatened, but Demetrius understands the deeper nature of what is at stake. If Artemis is proved to be powerless and worship to her is shown to be futile, the entire fabric of Ephesian society will come undone. Robbing Artemis of her divinity will rob the Ephesians of their powerful standing as her "temple sweepers," shifting the balance of influence in the area.

Here, in one snapshot, we have a picture of the spiritual battle raging all around us. We serve whoever we worship. While Demetrius's concern seems to be primarily economic, he understands that our wallets are a terrific indicator of who or what we worship. We spend money on things that are important to us. We invest in what we see as valuable. We sacrifice our resources for what we deem as worthy.

Write Matthew 6:21. How do these words help us see the connection between our wallets and our worship?

If someone only had access to your checkbook, what could they tell about your heart and your worship?

Demetrius accurately diagnoses the impact of Jesus on the hearts and lives of those who follow the Way, providing us with an excellent mirror with which to see the effect of Jesus in our own lives.

Referring once again to Acts 19:23-27, note the different ways that Demetrius describes the impact of the Way on the hearts of the people of Ephesus. Some of the effects are overt and some are implied by the actions and choices of the Christians. Use the change you see in their lives as a way to examine the impact of Jesus in your own life.

The Impact of Jesus	
Ephesians	*My Heart*
Their priorities?	My priorities?
How they spent their money?	How I spend my money?
Where they invested their time?	Where I invest my time?
Where they put their confidence?	Where I put my confidence?

The authority under which they lived?	The authority under which I live?
What they spoke about to others?	What I speak about to cthers?

This is one of the most remarkable passages of the powerful impact that the message of Jesus has on the hearts of those who commit themselves to Him. It reveals the penetrating nature of the cross. Once it enters our lives, it touches and transforms every piece of our hearts. So deep is the effect of the good news of Jesus on the hearts of the Ephesians that the businesses who make their profit from sin find their economic security in jeopardy. They can't make a profit because so many people have shifted their focus and confidence from the goddess to the Lord. People are no longer spending time or money on Artemis and her promises. Their confidence now rests in God, rather than an idol made of silver, stone, and wood. They let the footsteps of Jesus mark the path they walk, rather than following the directions of the priests of the goddess. The message of Jesus spreads like wildfire as people tell their neighbors, coworkers, friends, and family about the Immeasurably More life Jesus has in store for them.

The impact of Jesus should be as dramatic in our lives as it was in the lives of the Ephesians. Jesus must shape and define our priorities. The cross directs our focus away from self to seeking first His kingdom and His righteousness. Our redirected priorities find their best realization in the places where we choose to invest our time and money. We no longer pay for the movie or song that uses profanity or immorality for entertainment. We let Jesus influence the time we spend in front of the television. We build our lives on the truth of His Word, rather than placing our confidence in the latest media report or scientific discovery. Even the things we talk about are shaped by the person of Jesus. His ways, His standard, His love, and His grace change the way we interact with others, even as His faithfulness and mercy mark the path we walk.

It'll Do Lane

The best place to live is in the place that doesn't rock the boat. After all, nobody wants to be seen as different or a "fanatic." I will keep my faith private so as not to make anyone uncomfortable.

Immeasurably More

The world will notice when I make the move into Immeasurably More. What happens in my heart has an impact on those around me. The deeper I let the cross move in my life, the more dramatic the difference in the way I interact with the world.

Choosing a Home For Your Heart

It'll Do Lane is best defined by a desire to stay comfortable. Its pull is magnetic. The move into Immeasurably More requires a risky move of faith. It will change everything, and change is never comfortable or clean. Read Galatians 2:20. Let Paul's words help you make a resolution to leave It'll Do Lane and take up residence in God's Immeasurably More.

Day 3

Have you ever moved? We moved several years ago. It wasn't a dramatic move. We moved within the same city, just changing neighborhoods. What is amazing is the way it impacted every part of our lives. Moving changed where we walked, the roads on which we drove our cars, where we shopped, the people with whom we shared a fence and a friendship, and where we spent our money. We no longer invested time or energy in our old house. We concentrated our attention on our new home. Everything about our lives changed because we moved six miles.

The same is true of the move from It'll Do Lane to Immeasurably More. Leaving It'll Do will require learning new routes, walking in new paths, discovering new shops, meeting new neighbors, finding new outlets for joy and celebration, and rearranging our environment. We will find that some of our old stuff doesn't fit in our new home. It needs to go. We will find other things that we need to bring into our lives in order to best enjoy our new home.

When you physically move, you send out change of address cards. They declare without reservation that we no longer live at our old address. It is no longer the residence of our hearts. We ask others to share our joy in making a new house our home.

Immeasurably More

Write II Corinthians 5:17 in your own words, making it your moving announcement.

The charges that Demetrius raises against Paul enrage the crowd gathered to listen to him. They rush as one man to the Great Theater in Ephesus, an immense structure that holds up to twenty-five thousand people.[3] The confusion and loud exclamations spur a mob mentality which draws the people of the city into the theater. They drag two of Paul's traveling companions into the center of the riot. Paul wants to go in and address the crowd, but the leaders fear for Paul's life and restrain him. Inflamed by local pride and fervor for the goddess, the mob cries out with one voice for two hours, "Great is Artemis of the Ephesians!"

Finally, the town clerk is able to quiet the crowd. He points them to the grandeur of the temple and the place Ephesus holds as the keeper of the goddess. He directs Demetrius to take Paul to court if there is a valid charge to bring against him, while noting that the men have done nothing wrong. In the end, he reminds them that Rome is watching. Any move of unrest or incivility will bring the wrath of the Empire on their heads and threatens their status as a free city.

Paul and his companions are able to safely make their way out of the city.

The riot in Ephesus shines a light on the obstacles and challenges that we will face as we make a move into God's Immeasurably More. The world is content for you to stay on It'll Do Lane. When we live in It'll Do rather than Immeasurably More, the world has a stake in our lives that it will not easily give up. It will put up a fight, doing its best to intimidate you and make you feel like It'll Do Lane is the best you can do.

Write John 16:33.

The obstacles the world puts in our path are big. They are embedded in the political, economic, cultural, social, and religious forces of our day. They can be the kind of things that look too big to fight, too overwhelming to do anything about, and too powerful to stand against. Making the move to Immeasurably More demands that we measure these big forces against the heart of our big God. We have to remember that the Lord has called us to the Way. In following Jesus, we rely on Him to meet the forces that threaten to keep us on It'll Do Lane.

Obstacle #1 – *Under whose authority will you live?* The political forces of any society stand as a source of authority and rule in our lives. Christians live with the unique obligation to live in submission to the governing authorities while bowing to the sovereignty of God. The world will try to convince you that the political arena should have the final authority in our lives, having the right to legislate our faith as well as our civil actions. In order to live in God's Immeasurably More, we must have a very clear view of the One whose authority directs the course of our lives.

Read Acts 5:29 and I Timothy 2:1-4. How will we respond to the political forces in our society as we learn to live the Immeasurably More life?

Obstacle #2 – *On whom will you depend?* The economic forces in our society are powerful. Money controls everything. The desire for money fuels much of the action, positioning, and attitudes of our world. Money offers a comfort zone that sells the idea that if we invest ourselves in making money we will be able to make our own choices and control our own destinies. At the heart of these economic forces is a fundamental question about dependence. Will I rely on myself to take care of me or will I depend on God to provide more than I can ask or imagine?

Read Matthew 6:25-33. How does dependence on God lead us to living in His Immeasurably More?

Obstacle #3 – *By which standard will you live?* The cultural forces in our world are unique. There is tremendous pressure to conform to the standards laid out by the culture. Acceptance of sin, calls to conform to what "everybody is doing," the promotion of truth as relative and individually determined, and the belief that personal satisfaction is the greatest good are subtly woven into the messages that bombard us every day. Living in God's Immeasurably More calls us to live by the constant standard of Jesus, rather than the changing preferences of the world.

Read John 13:15 and I John 2:6. Look up the word *standard* in the dictionary. How does its definition help us understand the call to Christlikeness?

Obstacle #4 – *With whom will you find connection?* We are social creatures. God declared from the first days that it was not good for man to be alone. He made us to live in relationships and share our lives with others. Our society uses peer pressure to try to force us into its mold. Our connections direct our hearts, our eyes, and our minds. Much of the sin in the world stems from a desperation to answer the need for connection in our lives. God longs for you to find your best, deepest connection in Him and through Him. It is the only way to live in His Immeasurably More.

Read II Corinthians 6:16-18. What kind of connections does God offer you when you live in His Immeasurably More?

Obstacle #5 – *Whom will you serve?* We live in a religious society. There is great interest in spirituality and a longing for answers for the soul. The world offers many paths that claim to open a way into the divine. Our culture tells us to pick one. Any one will do. What we choose to worship is the most defining thing about us. Where we put our faith shapes how we see ourselves, others, our circumstances, our struggles, and our blessings. The world tells us that we can divide our worship, invest our faith in any number of avenues, and serve anything as long as we serve ourselves. God knows that we will never thrive until our hearts are completely committed to Him.

Read Matthew 4:10 and Matthew 22:36-40. How will investing our hearts in God alone open the door into His Immeasurably More?

These obstacles are so much a part of our world that we can't help but be touched and shaped by them. A large part of learning to leave It'll Do Lane and move into God's Immeasurably More is learning to recognize the pressure that is brought to our lives, call it by its proper name, and listen to God's answer to the ideas that it promotes as inevitable and unchanging. The world may riot as you make the move away from It'll Do Lane. It may challenge you and shout its "great" ideas with a loud voice. But just like Paul, God will provide a way of escape. Walking in the Way is the only way out of It'll Do and into Immeasurably More.

Day 4

Having faced a city-wide riot, Paul leaves Ephesus and settles in Macedonia for three months. We have one more recorded encounter between Paul and the Ephesian Christians in Acts. On his way to Jerusalem, Paul stops in the Ephesian port city of Miletus and calls for the Ephesian elders to come for a time of instruction and blessing.

Read Acts 20:17-38.

How does Paul describe the way he served among them?

What did he declare among them?

What warning does he give these men?

What blessing does he leave the Ephesian church?

There are many wonderful lessons that shine from Paul's emotional encounter with the Ephesian elders. He describes the responsibilities of the shepherds of God's church, communicating the deep need to watch over the flock of God's people and be watchful for those who would come in to ravage the family God loves.

These words also contain a snapshot of the Immeasurably More life. Paul draws their eyes back to the way he lived among them in order to give them a clear picture of the Immeasurably More God wants to create and shape in their own lives.

Immeasurably More

Can someone look at your life and see God's Immeasurably More? Explain.

Read again Acts 20:18-21. How does Paul describe his actions and the heart he lived out with the Ephesians?

The Immeasurably More life comes into clear focus as we examine the way Paul lived while in Ephesus. As he describes his time with them and reminds them of the truths of God, he gives them a living example of the Immeasurably More God wants to work in their lives. Paul understands that the lives others see us live become signposts that point others to Jesus. The Immeasurably More life is not lived in a closet or only within our private moments with God.

The richness of the Immeasurably More life is something that will spill over into our relationships, be evident in our activities, be seen in our attitudes, and overflow into our conversations, interactions, and the way we walk through the joys, struggles, and ordinary, everyday moments of life.

Paul begins be reminding them that he lived among them as one who was **serving the Lord**. **Humility** defined his attitude, even as his tears revealed his **tender heart**. He faced the trials he encountered with **perseverance**. He spoke with **courage** and **conviction**, living out God's **purpose** with resolve. He spent his days **pointing others to Jesus**, the power of the cross, and the remarkable transformation God has in mind for all of us.

Read Acts 20:22-27. How does Paul describe his actions and the heart he lived out with the Ephesians?

Paul goes on to draw their eyes to the relationship He shares with the Lord. He describes a life **dependent on God** and **guided by His Spirit**. He exhibits a heart of **deep surrender** and **overwhelming peace** as he relates the things God has revealed to him about what lies ahead in Jerusalem. Paul has a remarkable **focus**, longing to pour out the message of Jesus and His grace. He exhibits **integrity** and **walks in the whole counsel of God**.

Read Acts 20:28-32. How does Paul describe his actions and the heart he lived out with the Ephesians?

As Paul shares the wisdom of God with the Ephesian elders, he reminds them of the way God has worked in their lives. He is **able to trace the fingerprints of God**, speaking to them with **care** and **concern** for their safety and welfare. He was **earnest** and **dedicated** to sharing the full message of the cross with those he loved. He speaks a **blessing** into their lives, putting them in God's hands and reemphasizing the wonderful things God wants to do in them and through them.

Read Acts 20:33-38. How does Paul describe his actions and the heart he lived out with the Ephesians?

Paul's **contentment** was evident to the Ephesians as he **took care of the needs of others** as well as his own. He was committed to **working hard**, applying the full force of the cross to everything he did. He was a man of **compassion** who noticed the weak. His heart overflowed with **generosity**. He found **joy** in **living out the words of Jesus**.

The Immeasurably More of Paul's life bubbles up as we see him kneel down and **pray** with those he loves and treasures. He is **deeply connected** to others, opening his heart to them in **friendship** and **transparency**. He **walks with others**, always leading them deeper into the life God means for each of us.

In the Paul's Heart space to the right, write in all the characteristics of Immeasurably More that we noted in bold during this day's study. Use this moment to capture the big picture of the life God wants for you.

Immeasurably More

Now you need two pens of different colors. In the My Heart space to the left, use one pen to write in the Immeasurably More characteristics that you feel God is already working to bring to fruition in your life. Use the other color to note the elements you want to ask Him to make real in your life.

In Paul, we get an amazing glimpse into the life of someone devoted to living in God's Immeasurably More. Paul's life frames the richness, abundance, and depth that God empowers us to live. This is the life God wants for you. This is the life you were made to live.

The Immeasurably More life is for apostles and super saints. I am just regular, ordinary me. God doesn't want to work in me like that. I am comfortable where I am.

God has something planned for me beyond what I can ask or even imagine. There is a rich, sweet life waiting for me in Jesus. I believe God can and will work in my life to create His Immeasurably More in me for His glory.

Taking a step into the Immeasurably More life will change you forever. It will have a deep impact on those around you, the way you see the world, and the paths you walk from this moment forward. There will be obstacles to face, riots to endure, and joy to be experienced. Are you ready to learn how to walk in God's Immeasurably More?

[1] *NIV Study Bible*, p1687, *Archaeological Study Bible*, p2036
[2] Conybeare & Howson, p465
[3] *NET Bible*, p2035

Immeasurable Love
Lesson 3

Some of the most powerful lessons we can ever learn about God are found in the words and simple melodies of the songs that we teach our children. "Jesus Loves Me" holds a deep truth that has the power to fill today with joy, soothe your soul with peace, and bring perspective back to distracted eyes, rest to a soul weary with worry, and direction to feet that don't know which way to turn. The Bible resonates with the message that Jesus loves you. Every page points to His heart. Every action highlights His passion. Every word echoes with His heartbeat. He loves you. That love is the bedrock of faith, the fuel of transformation, and the framework for living in His Immeasurably More. Sing "Jesus Loves Me" today. Sing it out loud. Sing it on your way to work. Sing it in the car. Sing it in the shower. Sing it and be sure – "Jesus loves me, this I know."

Day 1

The Book of Ephesians is a powerful letter written to point Christians toward the Immeasurably More life. Jesus doesn't want us to settle. He doesn't want us to take up residence on It'll Do Lane. In fact, He died on a cross to make sure that you had access to everything God's Immeasurably More means for your heart. He wants you to embrace the life you were made to live. A life of abundance, fullness, purpose, peace, and joy.

He wants you to live in the deep ocean of God's love, experience His expansive grace, be strengthened by His limitless power, and have a rich enough faith to dream God-sized dreams.

Immeasurably More

This is the life God has always wanted for His people. He wanted it for the Ephesian Christians who first received this letter. He wants it for you, as you read Paul's epistle two thousand years later. He wanted it for Adam and Eve in the Garden of Eden. His design since the first waking hours of creation has been to give the people He loves an Immeasurably More life. Also since those early moments, it has been man's tendency to settle for less than God's best for us.

Read Genesis 2:4-9, 15-25.

Describe the home God created for Adam.

Describe the work and purpose that God gave Adam to do.

What specific command did God give to Adam?

Who did God give to Adam to share in this abundant life?

The pages of the Bible open with a panoramic view of God's power, wisdom, and creativity. Light permeates the new world, while seas are being pulled back, mountains are being stretched, and valleys are being dug. Lush vegetation covers the ground as the sky fills with wings and the sea teems with a stunning array of life. Stars are set like diamonds in the velvety night. The moon calls the tides of the oceans. The lion roars. The elephant trumpets, and the bunny rabbit wiggles his nose.

The crowning glory of this creation is man. God forms man from the dust of the earth, breathing in the breath of life and making him both substance and soul. Created in the very image of God, man walks in the garden of God's delight. He lives fully in God's presence and His purpose. God gives the man a woman with whom to share the journey. God fills every need, opens every door, answers every longing, and surrounds man with every beauty.

In what way is the Garden of Eden a picture of the Immeasurably More life?

Have you ever imagined what it might have been like to live in the Garden of Eden? No bills, no laundry, no pink slips, no deadlines, no worries, no stress, no long lines, no pain, no illnesses, no alarm clocks, and no guilt. Walking with God every day, they lived in the fullness of His delight. They experienced all the wonder of seeing His glory. They talked with Him, learned His heart, enjoyed His favor, and walked continually in His presence. They understood His purpose, lived under His care, and trusted His goodness. There was no shame, guilt, doubts, sin, or barriers. God opened His arms and His heart and invited them into Himself. Adam and Eve, for a while, lived the Immeasurably More life.

Read Genesis 3:1-24.

How does the serpent tempt Eve into accepting less than God's best?

Describe the emotions Adam and Eve now feel because they walked outside of God's purpose for them.

What does God provide for Adam and Eve even as they walk away from the Immeasurably More life?

This one snapshot captures the heartbreak of settling for something other than God's Immeasurably More. Tempted by the serpent, they choose to leave the garden of God's delight and take up residence on It'll Do Lane. In that moment, Satan makes It'll Do sound like a grand place to live. He still does.

We will be using Adam and Eve as a touchpoint to help us examine the temptations we face, the choices we make, and the consequences that we endure when we settle for It'll Do Lane. Even as we watch them leave, God makes us all a promise that Immeasurably More is still possible. He will provide a way. He will overcome the obstacles. He will issue an invitation. He will pay the immeasurable price so that our hearts can experience the Immeasurably More He created us to have.

Day 2

In Ephesians, there is a beautiful picture of the Immeasurably More life to which God calls us. It is a life defined by Jesus, lived in Jesus, and empowered by Jesus. The cross is the central point for this abundantly full life.

Each section of the first three chapters of Ephesians adds another brushstroke to the portrait of God's Immeasurably More. As we walk through each section, we will see the more God calls us to and the temptations to settle that hinder our way. The last three chapters of Ephesians are a roadmap into the Immeasurably More life. They teach us how to walk in all the delight God has in His heart for us.

Read Ephesians 1:1-6.

How does God describe the connection between God and Jesus?

How has God blessed us?

When did God choose you? For what did He choose you?

How does God connect us to His heart?

What is the ultimate purpose of the Immeasurably More life God gives us through Jesus?

These opening words of Ephesians should make us smile. Paul wastes no time pointing us to the heart of the Immeasurably More life. The foundation of the extravagant abundance God wants for you and me is rooted in the relationship He offers our hearts. He wants you to be His child. He wants to share the same relationship with you that He shares with Jesus. He wants to be your Father.

When we become His children in Christ, He pours out every spiritual blessing. All of the richness, joy, contentment, satisfaction, and purpose that He has in store for you is mined in the person, work, call, and heart of Jesus. God breathes His blessings into our lives in the same way that He breathed the breath of life into Adam. These blessings are what animate the Immeasurably More life within us.

Name five blessings that are yours today because you are in Christ.

Take a look in the mirror. You have been chosen by God. He picks you. He wants you. He longs for you to rest in His arms, find delight in His heart, and make your home in His presence.

He chose you before the foundation of the world. He looked out over the vastness of history and time, and settled His eyes on your face. Because of you, He moved in history, making a plan, and designing a destiny for your soul. Your destiny, the best path for your heart, is found in being a child of God. Adoption opens the floodgates of heaven.

What does it mean to be adopted?

Pregnancies can be unplanned, but adoptions never happen by accident. When you are adopted, you are chosen – deliberately, thoughtfully, purposefully, and intentionally. Adoption sets its heart on relationship. Only the richness of deep connection will do.

Through Jesus, you have been adopted into the family of God. You belong. You have a place. You fit in His heart. He works in your life to make you into the image of His Son. Holiness shapes your steps. The purpose of His will finds its best expression when you decide to live chosen. All of God's Immeasurably More comes to fruition when, as His children, we are able to live lives that praise His glorious grace.

How do we live chosen?

Adam and Eve were chosen. God created them to be the first members of His family. He connected them to His heart, loving them beyond measure. He walked with them, provided for them, cared for them, and created a world in which they could dwell in His presence.

What did they choose instead of living chosen and connected to God?

The opposite of choosing to live within the relationship God wants to give us in Christ is to choose to live independently. We decide that we can do it ourselves, go our own way, and do what we want to do. We settle for walking on our own, rather than walking with God.

Read Luke 15:11-32.

How do each of the sons choose to live independently rather than living in connection with their father?

How does the father invite both sons to live chosen?

Sometimes I am defiant like the prodigal son. I take all the rich extravagance of my blessings and waste them in a personal bid for independence. I want to set my own path, live by my own standard, and experience the "freedom" that comes from choosing for myself. More often, I am like the older brother. I let pride, jealously, self-pity, and self-focus rob me of the sweetness God wants to share with me. He calls me in, but I cross my arms and choose to stand just outside. I hear the music and joy of others, while letting bitterness define the rhythm of my soul.

Living chosen means that we stop jumping through the hoops the world sets up as tests of belonging and choose to live in the truth that we are God's beloved. We set our feet on a path towards home, accepting His grace and the love He longs to lavish on us. Living chosen means choosing to be humbled by the Father's invitation to come inside, rather than being stubborn and determined to create our own joy.

How will you deliberately live chosen today?

It'll Do Lane

You can't live on It'll do Lane without setting up a perimeter of independence. God can come into certain parts of the neighborhood, but other places are strictly off limits. They belong to me, and I will choose how to live in those spaces.

Immeasurably More

I am chosen by God Himself. He planned for us to be together before the foundation of world, making a way for me to be adopted into His family. Choosing to live in connection with God unleashes all the spiritual blessings God has in store for me in Christ.

Choosing a Home For Your Heart

Today will be filled with a myriad of choices. At the root of each one will be the same question – My way or God's way? Each time we choose "my way," we settle our hearts a little more deeply on It'll Do Lane. Each move of surrender to God's way moves our hearts further into His Immeasurably More. Commit today to being very aware of your choices and the direction they are taking you. Choose to live chosen.

Day 3

Living fully in the relationship of love God offers us means that we must first acknowledge the ways in which our actions and choices disrupt the intimacy and joy He longs to share with us. Sin leaves our relationship with God broken, which breaks the heart of God. It plants us firmly on It'll Do Lane. But God doesn't want us to live there. God measured the power of sin against His immeasurable love and invites us to live forgiven.

Read Ephesians 1:7-10.

Define *redemption*. How is that we have redemption?

By what measure does He forgive our trespasses?

How is the will and purpose of God made known through Jesus?

What is the purpose of God's plan?

In order to appreciate the riches of His grace, it is necessary to understand the seriousness of sin. Sin is not just a little wrong. It isn't a mistake or a miscalculation. Sin is rebellion against the holiness of God. It is the determination to walk in our own way, follow our own desires, and set our own paths. It is the defiant act of a heart that looks at God and says, "No."

We are good at dressing sin up to hide its ugliness. We like to spin garments of rationalizations and illusions of good intentions to cloak our sin and ease our minds. We justify our behavior. We convince ourselves that tomorrow will be soon enough to surrender. We make excuses, and judge ourselves by the evil around us. As long as we are "better" than our neighbors on It'll Do Lane, we tell ourselves that we are okay.

God doesn't hide the nature of sin from us. He doesn't sugarcoat it or whitewash its consequences. If we are going to live in His Immeasurably More, we are going to have to face the reality of sin. The good news is that we don't face it alone. God knows better than we do how sin destroys the relationship He wants to share with us. He understands the brokenness it leaves behind. He sees the chains and cement boots it binds to our souls.

His answer for sin, and all of its ugliness, is revealed in Jesus. Through His blood, we have redemption. Redemption means that God pays the cost to set us free. He moves in love to answer the tragedy that holds our souls captive. He forgives our trespasses and washes away our sins, making us new, whole, clean, and holy.

How has God lavished His grace on you?

Grace is God's answer to sin. The cross is the exclamation point that declares how much He loves you. The blood of Jesus is the remedy for the brokenness and chaos that overwhelm our souls.

At the perfect time, God's will and purpose were revealed in Jesus Christ. The cross marked the culmination of a plan that had been set into motion before the foundation of the world. Christ's sacrifice unites our hearts to the heart of God. It bridges the gulf created by our sin and opens the door into His presence.

It seems so simple. Given a choice between sin (with all of its guilt, shame, and heartache) and forgiveness (with its richness, peace, and joy), it seems like a no-brainer to walk straight into the forgiveness that Jesus paid for on the cross, and not look back. But too many times, we hang onto the baggage of It'll Do Lane. We let guilt and shame define where we live, letting it rob us of the Immeasurably More God created for us.

Read Genesis 3:7-10. Make a list of the impact sin had on Adam and Eve.

Vulnerability, self-reliance, fear, shame, and guilt. Sound familiar? Sin has the same impact on our hearts today as it did back in the Garden of Eden. Even as we live as children of God, we struggle with the residue of sin. Washed clean, we have a hard time laying down the guilt, fear, and shame that attached itself to us when we disobeyed God.

On a scale of 1 – 10, how much do you struggle with the weight of guilt robbing you of the Immeasurably More God wants for you?

Guilt rests its eyes on "I" – what I should have done, what I shouldn't have done, what I need to do now, how I can fix it, how it is impossible for me to fix it, how I failed, and the disappointment and grief I brought to the hearts of those I love.

Immeasurably More

In the immediacy of sin, guilt has a place. It brings an awareness of wrongdoing and is meant to turn our eyes to the only One who can help us. Guilt is designed to be the first step in a process that moves our hearts to the cross and into the grace of God.

Too many times we get stuck in guilt and never move beyond that point. We let the recording that plays in our heads get jammed in a continual replay loop, rehearsing our shame rather than rejoicing in His salvation. When we do that, we set up our residence on It'll Do Lane and decide to live there.

Read Hebrews 12:1-3. How do we learn to embrace forgiveness and let go of guilt?

Letting go of guilt is a three-step process.

First, we have to deliberately and intentionally lay guilt down. We have to make the decision not to let it control our thoughts and determine our direction. Put guilt and all of its baggage into the hands of Jesus. Leave it there. Don't take it back. Sometimes that is a minute-by-minute move of the heart. Each wave of guilt has to be purposely put in God's hands. Each time it comes up, it has to be met with the surety of His grace and the reality of His blood. Over time, it gets easier to hand those heavy bags over to Him.

Second, we have to fix our eyes on Jesus. Remember, guilt draws our eyes inward. If we want to live in His Immeasurably More, our eyes have to learn a different focus. Jesus is the founder and perfecter of our faith. He is the base line and the finish line. It is His faithfulness that allows us to live in His promises. It is His grace that allows us to dwell in His love. It is by His authority as the One seated at the right hand of God that sin is vanquished and guilt flees. It takes practice and concentration to learn a new focus, but letting Him fill our vision will eventually dissipate the distractions guilt produces.

Third, play something new. Record the truths of God's Word deeply in your heart. When the old guilt and shame recordings begin their droning, turn up the volume on God's voice. Recite Scripture. Read it aloud. Write it on a card and carry it with you. Psalm 103:10-13 is a great place to start. His Word is truth. It unveils the lies guilt likes to weave. His promises are sure. They will point you to stable ground. His love for you is unstoppable. His grace is bigger than your guilt.

Which of these steps do you most need to embrace today? How will you do that?

Day 4

God calls us into lives that declare we are chosen and that find deep joy in being forgiven. Living in His Immeasurably More challenges us to shed the independence that characterizes It'll Do Lane, and leave behind the baggage of guilt and shame that so often weighs down our hearts. As God shapes us and transforms us to walk in this abundant life, He gives us a special gift with a guarantee that teaches us how to walk with an assurance that defies the logic of the world.

Read Ephesians 1:11-14.

What do we have because we are in Him?

How does He work out His plans?

Ultimately, what is to be the fruit of our lives?

What prompts our belief and faith in Christ?

With whom are we sealed?

What kind of guarantee does He bring to our lives?

Immeasurably More

God is working within you. That is an amazing truth. It is stunning to realize that right now God is calling you, shaping you, and leading you deeper into the image of His Son. In Him, you are chosen. You have obtained an inheritance that comes with being His child and living as a part of His family. The things of this world do not hold the sum of our hope. We look forward to a day in which we will see His face and fall at His feet in worship.

God created this pathway for you from the beginning. The idea behind "predestined" is that God has a plan, a destiny if you will, that He longs for you to follow. He has built a path that will lead you straight to His heart. He has, however, made the sovereign choice to honor your free will. He gives you the right to choose where you will live – It'll Do Lane or in His Immeasurably More. But each day He is calling you, inviting you, and wooing you to live in His love and be completely His.

He is working all things according to the counsel of His will. Nothing can stop His purpose. No one can stall His plans. When we walk in His purpose, He moves in our lives to bring forth the fruit of praise. As we learn to look like Jesus, live in His character, and move with His nature, our lives begin to resonate with praise and shine with His glory.

How does your life praise His glory?

Hearing the word of truth opens the door of faith. The gospel – the good news about the life, death, and resurrection of Jesus – is the seed and light that allows the fruit of God's presence to grow in our hearts. In surrendering to that truth in baptism, we receive a very special gift and are marked in a very special way. We are sealed with the Holy Spirit. A seal is a mark of identification. It serves as a notification about who the Owner is and declares the privileges that go along with the seal.

The presence of the Holy Spirit in your life is God's seal. He marks you as His own. He claims you, openly declaring that you belong to Him. From the moment you rise from the waters of baptism, you are never alone. God is not only with you, He dwells within you. He walks with you, guiding you, encouraging you, interceding for you, and teaching you what it means to live in God's Immeasurably More.

Read Romans 8:9-17. How does the Spirit work in the lives of those who belong to Christ?

One of the most important functions of the Holy Spirit is that He serves as a guarantee in the lives of those who live for Jesus. We live in world that does not offer many guarantees. In fact, we will say that the only sure things are death and taxes. But God is in the guarantee business. What He promises, He delivers. What He says, He does. The Holy Spirit dwelling in our hearts is our guarantee from God. Heaven is our inheritance. Living fully in His presence is the hope of our hearts. Until the day we acquire possession of that inheritance, God gives us a guarantee that we can bank on. He comes to live with us until we can go to live with Him.

It'll Do Lane specializes in "as is," which means that we take what we can see and hope for the best. When we buy into "as is," we understand that flaws, imperfections, and hidden damage come with the package and that we are on our own when it comes to dealing with the fall out. "As is" is clouded by uncertainty, doubts, second-guessing, and the hope that we will at least come out even in the end. But this is not hope in its truest, purest, highest form. It is hope built on self-reliance and the illusion of being in control.

How did Adam and Eve trade God's guarantee for a life of "as is"?

Every day, Adam and Eve walked with God. Every day, they lived in the full measure of God's presence. Every day, they enjoyed the abundance of His blessings, the blanket of His provision, and the peace of His purpose. With one decision they decided to trade in God's guarantee for a life of "as is." They moved from the garden into a land of uncertainty, hard work, pain, and imperfection.

I love the fact that even as Adam and Eve choose "as is," God gives them a guarantee. He promises them Jesus, and with Him an opportunity to one day move back into the guaranteed, Immeasurably More life.

Living in God's Immeasurably More means living in the assurance of God's guarantee. We can set down the doubts, be certain, know for sure, and live in the confidence of being positive that God will do for you everything He has promised.

Write I John 5:13.

It'll Do Lane

Life is full of hard choices, and there are no guarantees. I do the best I can, take life "as is," and manage the baggage that piles up in my life by pushing it to the side and hoping I have the strength to carry it all.

Immeasurably More

I have a chosen, forgiven, sealed life in Christ. He has given me a guarantee of His faithfulness by giving me Himself. Today, I can live with assurance and confidence, laying the guilt of yesterday in His hands, certain that tomorrow will be all that He promises it will be.

Choosing a Home For Your Heart

Would you rather invest in a guarantee or buy "as is"? The difference really comes down to trust. Do you trust God to do what He says He will do? Do you believe Him or do you believe in what you can figure out for yourself? The Immeasurably More life demands making the daily decision to put yourself in His hands, rehearsing His goodness, and trusting His guarantee. Read Mark 9:23-24. The cry of the father is the prayer of anyone who wants to move from It'll Do into His Immeasurably More.

Immeasurable Power
Lesson 4

What is the most awesome display of power you have ever seen? Perhaps you have been overwhelmed by the thundering waters of a waterfall. Scientists have super computers that attempt to quantify the power released by the sun. The seemingly endless power of the ocean can capture our imaginations. The power of a tornado or hurricane can force us to move out of the way or pick up the pieces left in their wake. We are fascinated by power. We try to harness it, control it, use it, and even create it. Perhaps we are so enthralled with power because we struggle with powerlessness. We are aware of our weaknesses. We are mindful of the truth that our batteries run down and our strength dries up.

The greatest evidence of power was best seen on a hill in Golgotha and in an empty tomb of a nearby garden. Here the power of love was put on full display. The power of transformation was unleashed. The power of grace thundered across eternity. With the full display of God's power came a stunning opportunity. You can choose to live in that power. The power that held a Savior to the cross is yours for the asking. The power that rolled away the stone is available to you today. The folks on It'll Do Lane are fascinated by power, but powerless. Those who choose to live in God's Immeasurably More enjoy an infusion of power that makes all the difference.

Day 1

We have already seen that Paul uses his own life to point people to the Immeasurably More life. What is true in Acts is true in the Epistles as well. Interwoven into Ephesians, we watch Paul intersperse personal references that stand as teaching tools for how to live the Immeasurably More life. What a blessing! I am a hands-on learner. Studying theory is great, but lessons come to life for me when I can see them in action. This is how God uses Paul. His life becomes a picture of what Immeasurably More looks like in three dimensions.

Immeasurably More

Who do you know that lives an Immeasurably More life? What does their walk with Christ teach you about how to live in God's abundance?

I know someone who has built a home right in the midst of God's Immeasurably More. She shows me what it means to deliberately be a person of faith. She trusts God. Not in theory. In the really hard, dark moments of life, she shows me what it means to take God at His Word and live in the reality of His faithfulness. She is able to see God's hand at work all around her. She teaches me how to open my eyes to His presence. She has banished worry from her vocabulary, setting her heart to continual prayer, constant thanksgiving, and consistent worship. She is an ordinary person. She would be surprised to find these words being written about her, but she gives me a concrete picture of how to live this abundant, overflowing, walking-by-faith kind of life.

Read Ephesians 1:15-16.

What has Paul seen in the Ephesian Christians that points him to God's movement in their lives?

What two actions does Paul take as he hears about the hearts of the Christians in Ephesus?

How does the way Paul responds point us to the Immeasurably More life?

Faith and love become trumpets that announce the presence and work of God in the hearts of the Ephesian Christians. Their faith in the Lord Jesus is evident in the way they move through their days, the decisions they make, and the priorities they set. Their love toward all the saints heralds the transformative power of the love of Christ. Walking in faith and love gives those around them the opportunity to see God at work in their lives.

The way Paul responds to the faith and love he sees displayed in their lives gives us another step to take into the Immeasurably More life. Hearts soaked in the abundance of God, overflowing with the Immeasurably More He promises, are lives characterized by thanksgiving and prayer.

Prayer and gratitude are both tools God uses to reorient our eyes. Prayer draws us into His presence and helps us see Him, bow before Him, understand His will, surrender to His purpose, and open our lives to His power and love.

Gratitude makes our hearts soft so that the seeds of the Immeasurably More life will take deep root and bear much fruit.

Write I Thessalonians 5:16-18.

If you had to write these verses in It'll Do language, what would they say?

Rejoicing, praying, and giving thanks belong to hearts that dwell in God's Immeasurably More. It'll Do residents have a different kind of cadence. If we were writing instructions to help people live more comfortably on It'll Do Lane, these verses might sound like this. "Complain often, rely on no one, make a list of all that you are entitled to, following your own will."

That is exactly the temptation that the serpent laid out before Eve. He directed her eyes away from the bounty of God's blessings and told her that she was entitled to eat any fruit she wanted. He enticed her to question God's motives and complain about His boundaries. "Don't rely on God," he said. "Trust your instincts."

We live in an entitlement society. We spend a lot of time figuring out what the world owes us. We demand our way, that our desires be met, and that we be catered to. Don't believe me? Watch television for thirty minutes. We have determined that society owes us happiness, health, and comfort, and we whine when we don't get our way.

This entitlement mentality spills over into our spirits. We believe that God should make our lives easier. When we aren't comfortable, we reassess our commitment. Why should I give myself to God when He isn't giving me what I want? It sounds harsh, but the subtle reality of the entitlement mentality will keep us locked on It'll Do Lane.

Do you think you struggle with feelings of entitlement? In what way?

Honestly, I think we all fight the entitlement temptation. Gratitude is the antidote to entitlement's poison. Thanksgiving helps us see the continual movement of God on our behalves. It changes our perspective, focusing our eyes on our deep need and His overwhelming love.

How might deliberate gratitude help you live more fully in God's Immeasurably More?

What will you do this week to be more intentional about gratitude?

Day 2

Paul's thanksgiving for the Ephesian Christians overflows into a prayer that God will work abundantly in their lives. It is God who brings the Immeasurably More life into our hearts. It is His power that fuels that life to take shape in our hearts, expanding our vision, stretching our imaginations, and strengthening our faith.

Read Ephesians 1:17-18.

What does Paul ask God to give the readers of his letter?

How will knowing Him better affect the eyes of our hearts?

What Immeasurably More characteristic does Paul want us to know?

Gratitude and rejoicing for God's movement in their lives compels Paul to ask God to propel them deeper into His Immeasurably More. The next steps are embedded in coming to know more about God Himself. Paul asks that God empower those who seek His heart with a spirit of wisdom and revelation in the knowledge of Him. Paul wants us to have hearts that know God better, that trust Him more deeply, and respond to Him more quickly.

How do we get to know God better?

Growing in a spirit of wisdom and revelation means that our hearts become more tender to the truths of God. We see Him more clearly, we listen more carefully, and we surrender more readily. The process God uses to reveal Himself to us can be summed up by the letters – A-S-K.

Ask – The first step into a deeper spirit of wisdom and revelation is to ask God. If we want to know Him better, it is best to ask Him to reveal Himself to us. He promises that those who seek His face will find Him. He does not hide Himself from us. He wants us to know His heart, live in His will, and honor His holiness. He will work in mighty ways in a heart that desires to know Him.

Write James 1:5.

Study – The second step to getting to know Him better is to spend time in the revelation He has given us about Himself. The Bible contains the very best picture of God. It reveals His character, highlights His nature, spotlights His power, and underscores His holiness. The Scriptures contain everything we need to know to live in His Immeasurably More because it points us to Jesus. Bible study allows us to listen to His voice and enter into His presence. It gives us an up close look at His heart, and maps out the path into His overwhelming abundance. The best questions you can bring to any part of the Bible are 1) What do these words teach me about the heart of God? and 2) How do these words call me to live before Him?

Immeasurably More

Read Psalm 19:7-11. What benefits and blessings belong to the one who invests in studying God's Word?

Kneel – The third step into a greater knowledge of Him demands surrender. Wisdom involves knowing when and how to apply the principles of knowledge in our lives. In other words, it is not just about knowing the "what", but about putting that "what" into action. Kneeling before God is an act of humility. It opens our lives up to His power and asks that He do whatever is necessary to create the image of Jesus deep within us.

Read Luke 6:46-49. Draw a picture of the house that is built on God's Immeasurably More. Next to it, draw a picture of the house on It'll Do Lane.

Immeasurably More	It'll Do Lane

When the Word of God enlightens the eyes of our hearts, it shines a light on the great hope that is ours in Christ Jesus. It is a hope to which we are called. It flows out of the riches of His glory. It is a hope that reveals where we are going. It gives us light for the journey, and the confidence to embrace the abundant life for which we were made.

Residents of It'll Do Lane struggle with direction. Aimlessness and apprehension define their steps. Not knowing which way to go, we tend to listen to whatever voice can capture the attention of the crowd. Today it is one expert. Tomorrow another will rise up and point us down a different path.

Eve was headed in the right direction as long as she listened to the voice of God. When she started considering the words of another, she lost her direction and stumbled into darkness.

Knowing God better will stretch our hearts wide open for all the overflowing abundance He wants to pour into our lives. The better we know Him, the more certain we can be of the way He calls us to be His. The deeper we walk into wisdom, the clearer the path we need to walk becomes. The quicker we surrender, the faster we can experience His richness and power. The roadmap into His Immeasurably More isn't hidden or in a secret code. It is found within the heart of God Himself, and He gave us His heart in the Word. Open it up and see for yourself.

Write Psalm 119:105.

It'll Do Lane

I wish I knew which way to go. So many voices say so many different things, each promising me the happiness and comfort I deserve. Each path I walk down seems to turn into a dead end. I guess this is as good as it gets.

Immeasurably More

God uses the power of gratitude and prayer to make my heart sensitive to His presence. He gives me His Word as a light to open my eyes to His heart and to teach me to hear His voice calling me into hope. When I walk with Jesus, I am always going the right Way.

Choosing a Home For Your Heart

Keep a gratitude list this week. Get a piece of paper or a small notebook, and make brief notes throughout the day of things for which you are thankful. Keep track of blessings enjoyed, lessons learned, kindnesses received, prayers answered, comfort given, and joy experienced.

Day 3

I have a "do it myself" little boy. Do you know the type? He just has to find his own way. The best picture we have is of my son in front of a set of heavy glass double doors. On one side, my husband stands holding the door wide open. On the other side is our son, trying to push the closed door open with all his little might. His face is determined, his stance is set, and his resolve is unwavering. He is going to open that door himself, no matter what.

In what way does this moment capture the interplay between you and God?

Read Ephesians 1:19-21.

What is the next thing Paul prays that we will know about God?

Where is God's immeasurable power mostly clearly seen?

Where is Christ seated? How does this reveal His immeasurable power?

When we open our Bibles, it doesn't take very long to see God's power at work. Creation frames His power as mountains rise toward the sky, oceans take their place within His boundaries, stars fill the heavens, and the once empty earth bursts with life.

Walking with God's people gives us even more dramatic revelations of God's might. Plagues devastate the land of Egypt as God moves to set His people free. Water is piled in heaps as Israel walks on dry ground through the sea. Walls topple, giants fall, armies are halted, disease flees, demons shudder, and thousands are fed from a little boy's lunch.

Read Psalm 147:5. Why is it important to have a clear picture of God's abundant power?

The most dramatic demonstration of God's power takes place during the early dawn hours in a remote garden outside of Jerusalem. The resurrection of Jesus is the ultimate revelation of God's immeasurable power. In raising Jesus from the dead, death is conquered, fear is vanquished, sin is defeated, and Satan is overcome.

In rolling away the stone, God removes all the barriers that stand between us and His heart. He opens a pathway for us to live in His presence, rejoice in His redemption, and dwell in His deliverance.

The working of His great power helps us see Jesus at the pinnacle of authority. He is seated at the right hand of God with a name that is above every name. His sovereignty extends far above any rule, authority, power, or dominion that exists or will ever exist.

This is a stand-in-awe, bow-down, put-your-hand-over-your-mouth moment. When we can catch a glimpse of the immeasurable power of God it should move our hearts to humility and worship. But don't miss the direction of Paul's prayer. This power – this abundant, overwhelming, immeasurable power – is at work in you.

God doesn't reserve the working of His power for miracle moments and mountaintop demonstrations. He is willing to unleash that power in your life right now. The power that raised Jesus from the dead raises you to walk in a new life in Him. The power that rolled the stone away from the tomb will push through the obstacles that block your path into His presence. The power that gives Jesus the name above all names is yours as you wear the name Christian.

The working of His incomparable, immeasurable power is best seen in our lives in the transformation He longs to work within us. That power defeats sin, creates new life, knocks down walls, fells giants, opens new paths, and brings victory in you. Every time we see God at work with power, He is demonstrating what He is willing to do in your life.

Immeasurably More

Write Philippians 4:13.

The Immeasurably More life flows from living within the abundant power of God. Here is the problem. We tend to read this verse with a heart that says, "I can do all things with a little help from Christ." That is It'll Do thinking.

Remember the picture of my son and the door? The power captured in Philippians 4:13 is best seen in the way my husband was holding the open door. That is the picture of God you need to carry with you. Walk through the door He opens for you. Self-reliance is the only thing that will keep the power of God from flowing through your life. God will respect your choice to push on the closed door by yourself. In the end, however, you will have expended a lot of energy and not moved an inch.

How did Eve choose self-reliance over relying on God?

How does self-reliance keep you from living the Immeasurably More life?

Learning to rely on the power of God's Immeasurably More is a big decision played out in small moments. Learning to rely on someone grows as we get to know their heart. That is why Paul ties our understanding of the way His immeasurable power is at work within us to an increase in our knowledge of Him. The better we know someone, the easier it is to rely on them. The more time we spend with them, the better we know their character, the deeper our relationship with them, the more we trust them, and the easier it is to set our self-reliance down and let them work in our lives. It works the same way with God. The more we know about Him, the wider our eyes are opened to Him, the more we see about how He is willing and able to move in our lives, and the easier it is to let go of our self-reliance and let His power go to work within us.

Self-reliance is about more than exerting my own strength. It is about exerting my will. When I choose to push on the closed door, I am saying that I want to choose my own path, decide my own direction, and figure it out for myself. That is why the picture of Christ's authority is integral to the revelation of His power. Living in God's Immeasurably More always begins with surrender.

Think of a situation in your life right now in which you are struggling between living in God's power and doing it yourself. How might surrender be the key to experiencing His open door?

Day 4

I am not a very mechanically-inclined person. One day, my computer wasn't working, and I was frustrated. I had tried everything. I pressed buttons, flipped switches, opened drives, even sang it a song, but nothing worked. My computer and I spend a lot of time together, so I was feeling a little desperate by the time I called my husband. Now understand that my husband is a computer guy. No, really – it's his job. In fact, at work they call him "The Wizard." So it was with high hopes that I called him, expecting that out of his technical wizardry, he would be able to conjure the right sequence of buttons to push to make my computer come alive. He did. It was a little embarrassing. "Is it plugged in?" After a second of being defensive, I looked down under my desk, and sure enough, the cord lay innocently next to the power strip. I connected the cord, pressed the power button, and my computer sprang to life. "Always start with the basics," he said. "It is amazing how many times people think they have a big problem, when all they need to do is connect to the power source."

Paul prays that those who read his letter will be filled with power. He wants the power of gratitude to take deep hold in our lives and make our hearts tender to the truths of God. He longs for our eyes to be opened to the heart of God so that we can experience the rich hope to which He calls us in Christ. He lays out in full detail the scope of the power that is ours. Nothing less than the power of the resurrection is at work in our lives. Now, as he finishes his prayer, he reminds us of the necessity of being plugged into the power source.

Read Ephesians 1:22-23.

What power is there in the picture of everything being put under Christ's feet?

How is Jesus connected to the church?

What are the two pictures Paul uses to describe the church?

It'll Do Lane is filled with power. There are people, influences, forces, and governing authorities that all exert power in our lives. Media, friends, bosses, the government, money, peer pressure, society's standards, family, health, and even our own ambitions and desires have some measure of power. They strut their stuff in our lives, demanding that we invest ourselves in the power they offer. Each comes to us claiming to be enough power to get us through the dark places in life.

Paul points us to the truth. Jesus is the ultimate Power Source. All things have been put under His feet. That is a powerful picture of victory and authority. Jesus outshines all the other sources of power in this world. They are like birthday candles next to the sun.

Why are we tempted to plug into lesser power sources when Jesus offers us Himself?

Having placed all things under Jesus' feet, God raises our eyes and lifts our vision. Jesus is the Head of the church, His body. Connected to Him in the most intimate way, Christians live within the fullness of Jesus Himself. The Head animates the body. Without the Head, the body cannot function. The body cannot move on its own. It has no direction, no life, no power. Within the context of the Head, the body is alive with power and potential. It can grow, move, serve, love, and touch the world.

Read Colossians 2:18-19. Why is it essential to hold fast to the Head?

We cannot grow into the Immeasurably More life if we are disconnected from the body of Christ. We have to be plugged into the Head if we are going to live the abundant, full, rich life of God. We have to be engaged with the church in order to experience all of the Immeasurably More He wants to pour into our hearts.

So many people end up on It'll Do Lane because they want a connection with Jesus, but avoid His church. They invest themselves in the power sources of the world, but refuse to plug into His body. Being a part of the family of God means more than just showing up for an hour on Sunday morning, then scooting out the back. It means opening your heart to the people who make up His body and sharing your life with them. Accountability, transparency, love, compassion, and modeling Christ flow from being connected to other Christians. Together we sing, serve, study, and seek His face. We help each other experience the presence of God and imitate His Son.

How well connected are you to the body of Christ? What can you do this week to help someone else plug into the family of God?

In addition to a body, the Holy Spirit describes the church as the fullness of Christ. That is a beautiful picture. Embedded in the Greek word for fullness is a picture of a ship.[1] It is a ship that is filled to the rafters with all the good things Jesus can pack into the vessel. It has everything that it needs to make a successful voyage through this world. The church travels as the fullness of Christ through the world, inviting others to join in the journey.

Jesus fills His church with Himself. We embody all of His grace, love, glory, holiness, mercy, purity, and purpose as we walk in this world under His authority and by His power.

We travel through this life as the fullness of Him, who fills all in all. In Him, we will lack nothing. The power will never dry up, run out, falter, or go on the blink. There are no energy shortages or rolling blackouts in Christ. We just have to stay plugged in.

It'll Do Lane

Our society values people who can do it on their own. I want to be that kind of person – go my own way, blaze my own trail, and rely on my own strength. I don't want to have to depend on anybody. I just don't understand why I am so tired.

Immeasurably More ↑

God wants to unleash the immeasurable greatness of His power in my life. His power calls me to experience the fullness of His presence within the community of His people. The Immeasurably More life is a life plugged into Christ.

Choosing a Home For Your Heart

Every day I have the opportunity to choose my power source. I can tap into the power offerings of the world – fame, money, popularity, ambition, or status – and hope that they are enough to get me through the day. Or I can board the ship and live in the full power of Jesus. Where will I plug in today?

[1] Strong's, G4138

Immeasurable Grace
Lesson 5

What did you want to be when you were a kid? I love to watch little kids' faces when you ask them what they want to be when they grow up. Their eyes light up, grins stretch across their cheeks, and they share their dreams. No one settles when they are five. They imagine life as football players, doctors, astronauts, and ballerinas. They see themselves as super heroes, movie stars, and inventors. Children have the ability to dream big dreams and imagine big futures. They have no limits, and potential is just a word filled with possibilities.

The Immeasurably More life is, in many ways, about asking God what He wants you to be when you grow up. He dreams of a life for you that is beyond what you can ask or imagine for yourself. There are no boundaries on His blessings, or limits on His imagination. He never settles, or stops at It'll Do. He is willing to work in amazing ways in your life in order for you to be everything He wants you to be. Today is the day to see a little farther, stand a little straighter, and dream a little bigger. God's got plans for you.

Day 1

A picture of the Immeasurably More life is beginning to take shape. It is a life rich with the presence of God, enfolded in love, and empowered by His strength. Today God stretches our vision as He helps us imagine a life beyond It'll Do Lane.

Read Ephesians 2:1-3.

What was the state of the life you used to live?

Who did we follow?

Describe the life we all once lived.

Here is a clear and defining picture of life on It'll Do Lane. Underneath the glitzy veneer the world tries to paint of a life without God, the reality is grim. The spin doctors of the world try to tell us that life on our own is liberating, and pulses with the satisfaction of following our own course and our own desires. The truth is that life on It'll Do Lane is fueled by dreams that have died, shrinking imaginations, and souls that are so weighted down by sin, guilt, and shame that they can't imagine anything different.

In order for God to draw us into the Immeasurably More life, we must be honest about where we start. Even after we surrender to Christ, we are sometimes so hedged in by It'll Do thinking that we can't imagine a life much different than where we have always lived. God wants us to take the blinders off and see our lives from His perspective.

Direction

The It'll Do reality is first measured by the direction in which we walk. Walking in our trespasses and sins, we move down a dead end path. Sin poisons the soul. Trespasses describe a life of walking outside of the will and holiness of God. The ways of this world become familiar paths. They take on a routine quality as our hearts walk over and over again along their streets. The mapmaker for It'll Do Lane is the prince of the power of the air. He creates the maze that traps our souls and keeps us walking in circles that never lead anywhere.

Turning our eyes to the Immeasurably More life, the first thing that has to change is our direction. In fact, the transformation from death to life involves a definitive change in direction. It is called repentance.

Define *repentance*.

A repentant heart is essential for living the Immeasurably More life. Repentance literally involves changing direction. Where once we walked in the way of sin, repentance turns our hearts towards God and determines that we will walk in His way. It helps us renounce our allegiance to the prince of this world, and aligns our hearts with the King of Kings.

Repentance is not a one-time event. It is a state of the heart for those who long to live in God's Immeasurably More. Repentance makes our hearts tender to His voice, sensitive to His leading, and helps us seek His ways.

Read I John 2:6. What is the direction of a heart that lives in God's Immeasurably More?

Desire

The desires of a heart stuck on It'll Do Lane revolve around living out personal passions. Satisfying self, delighting in the desires of the body, and feeding the fantasies of the mind become the focus of those who settle for less than God's best. Satiating these desires takes the shape of small compromises in our lives. Rarely do we throw ourselves into the deep end of the pool of self-satisfaction. We dip a toe in and find it warm and comfortable. We move in a little deeper, find a little more pleasure, and eventually end up in over our heads.

Moving into God's Immeasurably More means allowing God to reshape our desires. This is probably one of the most difficult pieces of learning to leave It'll Do Lane. Our desires are what we want, what we think will bring us happiness, where we are most willing to invest our lives. To put those in God's hands and let Him transform our desires requires deep, daily surrender.

Read Luke 9:23. How will the steps Jesus lays out draw us into His Immeasurably More?

Identity

When we live on It'll Do Lane, we have an identity. We are one of the crowd, and by nature, children of wrath. When we follow our own direction and satisfy our own desires, we choose to stand in a place God wants no one to be. Sometimes we stand in the place for so long that we begin to believe this is all we can ever be. If children are told over and over again that they can't do math, guess what happens? They struggle with math. It doesn't matter if they test at genius level, what they are told trumps who they really are.

The world spends a lot of time telling you who you can be, who you will be, and who you are. It wants to define you by your limits, by what you don't have, and by who you can never be. The prince of this world knows that the message you allow into your heart will forever shape you, so he goes to extraordinary lengths to tell you that It'll Do is as good as it gets.

Here is the Immeasurably More truth – you are chosen by God, beloved by His heart, valued beyond measure, and treasured as His dear child.

He is willing to change your identity, the address of your heart, and the image of yourself that you carry with you each day. It requires learning to listen to a different voice, seeing yourself through new eyes, and walking away from the limits the world's lies put on your soul.

Read I Peter 2:9-10. How will learning to embrace this identity help you live in God's Immeasurably More?

Day 2

Have you ever just wondered where the time has gone? We live in a rushed world. Everything is flying at supersonic speed and we struggle to keep up, or, at least, from getting run over. Life seems to be a constant whirlwind. We don't even have time to breathe.

Sometimes I feel like I am so busy trying to keep up with my life that I don't have time to live my life. The living gets put on hold while I meet deadlines, handle emergencies, and juggle all the responsibilities on my plate. Life speeds by, and I feel like I have missed it.

The difference between living on It'll Do Lane and in God's Immeasurably More isn't the number of things on your list, the busyness of your schedule, or fullness of your calendar. The difference is found in whether or not you choose to fully live in today.

Read Ephesians 2:4-7.

Describe God.

Why is it important to have this clear picture of His rich mercy and great love?

For how long has He loved you?

What three specific things has He done for you?

Why has He done those things for you?

The Immeasurably More life must be defined by the heart of God. It is in Him that this amazing, abundant life takes shape. It is by His power that we can experience its richness. It is through His sacrifice and purpose that we can enter into His Immeasurably More. And it is in His character that we see the beauty of what He is creating within us.

God is rich in mercy. His mercy is described as rich in both senses of the meaning. He is rich in mercy in terms of limitless. He has a vast storehouse of mercy that He is willing to invest in me. I will never come to Him only to be told that there is insufficient mercy, that it is out of stock, or on backorder. God has deep pockets of grace.

His mercy is also rich in terms of fullness, vividness, and intensity. When we describe something as rich in this way, we are attempting to capture its texture and its impact. There is a luxury to His mercy that He extends to us. It captures an extravagance and depth that speaks to the deep needs of our souls.

Immeasurably More

What three words would you use to describe the richness of God's mercy in your life?

God's love is great. Again, the multiple layers of meaning for this word help us capture a glimpse of His love for us. It is immense, strong, wonderful, and extraordinary. His love is an immovable, unstoppable, immeasurable force that seeks to draw us closer and deeper into His heart.

It is within the context of God's rich mercy and great love that we have to see the next truth. While we were dead, God moved to bring us life. He draws us out of the darkness into His marvelous light. He breathes fresh life into decaying souls and creates a new, vibrant, living being. His grace raises us up into the resurrection life of Jesus. It is a life where death can no longer cast a shadow or exert a hold. It is a life meant to display the glorious colors of His beauty and showcase the exquisite nature of His heart. He seats us in the heavenly places in Christ Jesus, raising us above the mean, competitive, greedy, self-serving places we tend to make our resting places in this world. This seat gives us a new perspective on our lives and God's work in the world. He does all of this so that He might show us the immeasurable riches of His grace, pouring kindness into our souls in Jesus.

This is the life God wants you to live, the life He paid so dearly to give you. So why do we settle for so much less?

Read Genesis 3:16-19. Describe the life Adam and Eve had after they chose to settle for their way instead of God's Immeasurably More.

Pain, relationship problems, hard work, struggles and troubles, sweat, anxiety, scarcity, separation, and death. Sound familiar? That is life on It'll Do Lane. It is a shadow of the life we are meant to live, and we settle for the shadow rather than embracing the substance God says can be ours. We settle for just getting by, for making it through another day, for checking another thing off the list. We wish our days away, always hoping that tomorrow will be better than the life we have today. We walk around numb, looking up one day in surprise that life has passed us by.

God's Immeasurably More offers us the possibility of being fully alive right now. No matter our circumstances, the situation in which we find ourselves, or the struggles that swirl around us, God longs for us to soak in all of the abundance, beauty, wonder, joy, and dazzle of living life in Him.

It all starts with a commitment to live and be present in this moment. Don't wish it away, or walk blindly through it. Whatever you are doing, pay attention. God is here. He inhabits this moment of time. The fullness of His heart is invested in the space of today, as it will be in the space of tomorrow. Search for it. Seek Him out. He promises you will find Him.

Write Jeremiah 29:13.

Be sure that a God who is rich in mercy, great in love, and immeasurable in grace is looking and longing to flood your heart with His kindness. Be deliberate about experiencing the ways He expresses His love for you. Embrace the mercy He pours into your day. Watch for His kindnesses, and breathe them in deeply when you find them.

It'll Do Lane

I wish this day was over. I seem to be walking in a rut. Every time I try to chase a little happiness, I end up down a dead end street. Maybe tomorrow things will be a little bit better.

Immeasurably More

Today is alive with possibilities to meet God. As His child, He is reshaping my direction and desire. Every day brings a new measure of His mercy and kindness into my life. My heart is not limited by what I can see, but defined by what God sees in me.

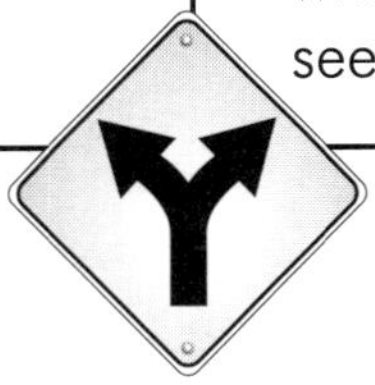

Choosing a Home For Your Heart

Make the choice to really **LIVE** today.
L – Look for Him. Seek His presence and look for His heart. He wants you to see it.
I – Invest in today. Don't worry about yesterday or tomorrow.
V – Value the beauty He plants in this moment.
E – Exercise your heart. Bow before Him. Stand in awe. Stretch your faith. Walk by His side.

Day 3

There is perhaps no more defining characteristic of the Immeasurably More life than grace. Grace is the reason we have the opportunity to live in God's Immeasurably More in the first place. Grace is the answer to our most desperate need. Grace offers us a pathway out of It'll Do Lane and into the arms of God. Grace is the power behind transformation, the light that pierces our deepest darkness, and the wings that give flight to joy.

Read Ephesians 2:8-9.

By what have you been saved?

Define *faith*.

In what way is grace a gift?

Grace is fundamental to the Christian experience. These words capture the essence of our need and the jaw-dropping, eye-popping, wow-inspiring reality of God's movement on our behalves. *"For by grace…"* reveals the pathway God opens up for us through the blood and body of Jesus Christ. Our sin cuts us off from the presence of God. It ruptures our relationship and ruins our hope. And it moves us straight to It'll Do Lane.

Grace is our only way to God. The blood of Jesus is the only way into salvation. The cross paid for our redemption. The empty tomb shouts the victory. Grace is God's great gift to us.

Write John 3:16.

Grace taps on our souls, inviting us, pleading with us, romancing us, and urging us to be reconciled to God. Faith is our answer to God's invitation. Faith opens the door for God to move in and work in our lives. Faith propels us to respond in obedience to His Word. Faith compels us to make a move of trust, a move of surrender, and a move of location. God's grace opens the door into His Immeasurably More. Faith lets us pick up and go.

In examining the connection between the invitation of grace and the response of faith, God makes a very clear note. We can't do it ourselves. It is impossible for us to solve the problem of our own sin. We can't do enough good, have enough right answers, reach deep enough, give sacrificially enough, or be holy enough on our own to break free from the penalty of sin. Depending on our works will keep us stuck on It'll Do Lane.

When we depend on our works, we are not depending on God. It becomes an exercise of control when the only answer is surrender. It springs out of fear when the only resolution flows from love. Works proudly declares that I have all the answers. Grace whispers in humility that Jesus is the only answer.

Grace demands that I lay my ambitious agendas, my self-made solutions, my ingenious ideas, and my proud posings at the feet of Jesus, seeing them for the pile of rubble that they are. Faith accepts that grace is possible, and that God is powerful enough, big enough, faithful enough, and loving enough to work the transformation in me that He says He will do.

In what way do you struggle with fully accepting God's grace?

In so many ways, this is what keeps so many of us on It'll Do Lane. I know. I lived there for a long time. I looked at my sin, caught a glimpse of God's holiness, and knew that I came up short. Instead of walking into grace, I decided I had to earn my place by His side. It was a sad, desperate, fearful time in my life. No matter how much effort I poured into good works, I knew in my soul that it wasn't enough. I lived on the edge of panic. Would God find me good enough or worthy enough to claim me as His own? What if I took a wrong step, thought a wrong thought, spoke a wrong word? I wanted to live in His Immeasurably More, but settled for something so much less. Pride and a desire to be in control locked me into It'll Do Lane. Fear, shame, and guilt kept me there.

Immeasurably More

With joy, I can tell you that God does not want us locked in a cycle of fear, works, and guilt. Jesus really is the answer. His grace is sufficient. His faithfulness is true. His Word is right. His love is deep. His power is vast, and His righteousness is sure. He promises to forgive every sin. He assures us that His blood is powerful enough to cleanse even the deepest stain. He declares that He will never leave us or forsake us. The question is, "Do we believe Him?"

Read John 6:28-29, writing verse 29.

Believe in Jesus. This kind of belief is not just head knowledge or an intellectual assent to a theoretical truth. Believing begins with the head, and then soaks down into the heart. It shapes our thoughts, and directs our actions. It molds our words, and compels our surrender. It is the decision to invest ourselves in grace. To believe that the impossible is possible in Jesus.

The decision to leave the guilt and weight of our own work is both freeing and difficult. It is a habit that must be broken, a way of thinking that must be reprogrammed. It requires the daily decision to believe in Jesus, to trust that what He says is true, to plant yourself in His grace and be still.

Spend the next few minutes in prayer. Quiet your heart in His presence. Pour out the ache of your shame. Ask Him to overwhelm you with His grace. Then listen to the words He has penned just for you.

II Corinthians 12:9

Romans 5:1-2

I John 3:19-23

Write the first sentence of I Corinthians 15:10.

Day 4

God's immeasurable grace has a tremendous, transformative influence in our lives. Grace gives us a vision of the life God wants us to live. It is a life made alive by His mercy and love. A grace-filled life guides our direction, shapes our desires, and defines our identity. It raises us up into a resurrection-empowered life in Christ, giving us a new perspective and a new address for our hearts. It frees us from the grinding guilt of depending on ourselves, opening our hearts to believe in Jesus as the answer to how to live an Immeasurably More life.

The full beauty of the immeasurable riches of His grace comes to fruition in our lives as we learn what it means to leave It'll Do Lane and take up residence in His Immeasurably More. There, we learn to embrace the life God has planned for us.

Read Ephesians 2:10.

Who are you?

Why were you created in Christ Jesus?

When did God initiate this plan for your life?

It is interesting how this verse parallels the three verses that started this section of Ephesians. In Ephesians 2:1-3, Paul describes life on It'll Do Lane. It is a life that is defined by death, sin, and shame. It is a life that follows the course of this world and walks in the ways of the prince of the power of the air. It is a life that focuses on satisfying self and meeting the desires and passions of the flesh.

Ephesians 2:10 is the portrait of a life lived in God's Immeasurably More. It is a life redefined and reshaped by grace. The richness of His mercy pours into our lives and His blood washes away all the selfishness, sin, and tendency to settle that we carry around with us. When we move into His Immeasurably More, His grace unleashes its full transformative power into our lives. It changes our identity, our desires, and our direction.

Identity

Because of His immeasurable grace, you are a new creation in Christ. Fresh, clean, and new because of the blood of Jesus, you shed the identity as a child of wrath and take on the identity of being a child of God. You belong to His family. You wear His name. You undergo a transformation that is creating a family resemblance between your heart and the heart of Jesus.

This new identity that we wear because of grace is beautifully wrapped up in the word *workmanship*. You are God's workmanship. He created and crafted you, lovingly working in your life to make you into exactly who He wants you to be. You are His masterpiece. You have not been mass-produced or rubber-stamped. His hand is on your life. He graciously molds you into the likeness of Jesus for His purpose and His glory.

The Greek word that we read as *workmanship* has in its root the idea of poetry.[1]

You are God's poem. Written by the Author of Life Himself, your heart is the verse by which He describes His love to the world. Your life is an expression of His beauty, a creation that gives those around you a glimpse into His heart.

How does it change your view of yourself to know that you are God's poetry?

Desire

A life created in Christ Jesus means that our desires are directed toward pleasing God. We long for His will to direct our steps. We look to His Word for clearer pictures of His nature. We seek to imitate His movement, embracing the holy and pure desires that define His character. We were created for good works, works that reflect the goodness of His heart.

Read Ephesians 2:3. In what kinds of works did we used to invest ourselves?

Remember that Paul is using verse 10 to compare and contrast the lives of those who live on It'll Do Lane with those who live in God's Immeasurably More. On It'll Do Lane, our hearts are focused on working to satisfy our own desires, follow our own passions, and act on our own dreams. When we move into God's Immeasurably More, our desires undergo a radical transformation. No longer do we seek our own desires; our greatest desire is to walk in His desires. The life we live, the things we do, the thoughts we think, and the roads we take are now all defined by His goodness and empowered by His grace. No more sinful, selfish, self-directed, evil, death-inducing works. We were created for good works – works that inspire praise, bring glory, reveal holiness, honor love, and value life.

Read II Corinthians 9:8. How does God's grace empower the working of good in your life?

Direction

God has been preparing for you to walk in His Immeasurably More since before the foundation of the world. He longs for His good, true, and righteous work to define who you are and direct where you walk. He wants us to walk in the path of this new, pure, holy life He has created for us in Christ Jesus. He does not want us to walk according to our own rhythm, but in cadence with the beating of His heart.

On It'll Do Lane, we followed the course of this world, letting it lead us wherever it wanted to take us. Listening to the voices of this world, we allowed the prince of this world to hold authority in our lives.

Living in God's Immeasurably More means that we follow in His footsteps, walk His paths, and listen to His voice. Since the time of Adam and Eve, God has had a plan for the people He loves. He created Adam and Eve in His own image. Their identity was rooted in looking like Him. Their desires were fully met in His provision. They walked in the good works He laid out for them.

How did eating the fruit change their identity? Their desires? Where they walked?

Every day we have the same choice as Adam and Eve. We can choose to listen to the voice of this world, following our own wisdom and our own desires. Our identity becomes warped by self-focus, our desires become twisted by personal passion, and our direction gets twisted. When we choose to follow that path, we choose to settle for less than God's best for us.

When we choose to walk in the richness of God's grace, we choose the Immeasurably More life. It is a life rooted in the person of Jesus, defined by His love, and empowered by His mercy. We become His poetry, created in Him for His glory and pleasure. We walk in His ways, do the good works He prepares for us, and define our purpose and passions by the desires of His heart.

It'll Do Lane

Salvation rests in the hands of those who work hard, do good, and act right. I know I can't measure up, but it's my trying that counts. If I work hard, hopefully God will see what I am doing and let me in. It is not enough, but it will have to do.

Immeasurably More ↑

I am saved by grace. Grace meets me where I am – full of sin, overwhelmed with shame, and governed by guilt – and opens the door into God's presence. As I respond to Jesus in faith, I surrender my life to Him. In obedience, I respond to the grace that invites me to be changed, rewritten, and made new.

Choosing a Home For Your Heart

My work or God's workmanship? Who do I want to be? I can choose to work in my own life, creating myself into who I think I need to be. Or I can walk in grace as God's workmanship, allowing Him to create the image of Jesus in me. Ultimately, this is a question of control and surrender. When I work, I am in control. When God works, He is in control. Take a moment to examine the fruit of the work in your life. Work done in your own power results in either pride or guilt. Walking in the grace of His good works brings humility, peace, and an ever-increasing awareness of God's presence into our lives.

[1] "poem"

Immeasurable Peace
Lesson 6

I used to love to play with building blocks – the kind that snap together and come in all different kinds of bright colors. I would sit for hours and build houses and castles, even whole towns. We had a bright green board that was the base, grass I guess in the best imaginations. From there, the building would begin. This kind of building has a rhythm. First, you lay the perimeter, leaving room for doors and entryways. Next comes the base. This is the most important part. Get the foundation wrong, and your house will tumble. Then it was time to move up the walls. If you were really talented, you could leave space for windows and do intricate designs with the blocks. Add a roof, and you had a house.

Every day you are building a life. You are adding pieces, making adjustments, fitting things together to make a home for your heart. The homes on It'll Do Lane are Do-It-Yourself kits. There are no instructions, just pieces that you are supposed to be able to put together and figure out how to make work. In God's Immeasurably More, you build with the Master Carpenter. He has a blueprint and a plan for the home He longs to build in your life. It is a beautiful place with bright windows, doorways into His blessings, and walls that are sturdy and thick. You are going to build today in one location or the other. Where do you want to live?

Day 1

Have you ever felt like you were in a hole you just couldn't get out of? You had dug yourself in so deep that there was no way to ever see the top? Those kinds of holes consume our lives. They destroy our confidence. Every day is a desperate attempt to find a way out. We grab any solution that promises an easy fix. Some days, it takes everything we have not to dig ourselves in any deeper. Finally, failure begins to define who we are. We try to make the hole comfortable. Maybe it won't be so bad. We give up hoping that it can be any different because hope hurts. We settle in for the long haul. It'll have to do.

Read Ephesians 2:11-12.

Make a list of the seven descriptions of life outside of Christ.

1.

2.

3.

4.

5.

6.

7.

It is quite a hole, isn't it? It'll Do Lane isn't a close enough, good enough kind of place. That is the lie that we sell ourselves in order to find a way to live there. It is the lie someone tells herself when she goes to buy one more thing she doesn't need and can't afford. The lie she whispers when she opens the bag and says, "I'll start on Monday." The lie that eases the twinge of guilt as she turns on the television to watch that show. The reality is that the hole is ugly. The hole is deep, and the hole is hopeless. We are so far in, there is no way out on our own.

"Therefore remember that at one time…" Paul calls us to take a good look at the hole we are in. Sometimes we can't find the resolve to leave It'll Do Lane until we see how bad it really is. In some circles, it is called hitting bottom. In Christ, it is called learning to look up.

Here is the reality of our hole.

1. Gentiles – Unable and unworthy to enter into God's presence to worship

2. Uncircumcised – Insensitive and unresponsive to the voice of God

3. Separated from Christ – Disconnected from His purpose and longing for our lives

4. Alienated from the commonwealth of Israel – Living outside of God's family, alone and lonely

5. Strangers to the covenants of promise – Unable to participate in joy or celebrate God's involvement in our lives

6. Having no hope – Defined by despair and discouragement

7. Without God in the world – Trying to do it on our own

Circle the number of the description above that best matches your hole.

Write Ephesians 2:13.

The most wonderful, amazing words in this verse are the first two. *"But now..."* The hole we find ourselves in is not the end of our story. The list above used to define our boundaries, mark the edges of our hope, and describe the reality of our hearts. But not now. Now Jesus is the answer. He lived in our holes, walked in our shoes, felt our pain, took on our shame, and cried our tears so that He could invite us into a different reality. So we could take His hand and climb out of the hole.

"Brought near..." Aren't those beautiful words? Far and near are opposites. They describe the extremes of the conditions of our heart. Because of the blood of Jesus, we aren't stuck in the hole. It doesn't have to be our reality. We can stay there. He won't make us leave. But He offers His hand and will empower us to take the steps we need to take to make a move out of the hole, if we want to go.

In the chart below, write the opposite reality that is ours because of the blood of Christ.

Far Off	Brought Near
Unable and unworthy to enter into God's presence to worship	Revelation 5:9-14
Insensitive and unresponsive to the voice of God	John 10:3-4
Disconnected from His purpose and longing for our lives	Romans 8:28-29

Far Off	Brought Near
Living outside of God's family, alone and lonely	I Corinthians 12:27
Unable to participate in joy or celebrate God's involvement in our lives	I Peter 1:8-9
Defined by despair and discouragement	Titus 2:11-14
Trying to do it on our own	Philippians 4:13

So here is the question to your heart. Where do you want to live? In the hɔle or with the Holy One?

Write Psalm 145:18.

Day 2

Peace is an elusive term. We crave peace, long for peace, and invest huge chunks of our heart in finding peace. Peace is almost as basic a need for our lives as wcter and food. Without it, our souls shrivel. There is a restlessness to our days that allows fear, cynicism, and bitterness to build up in our lives. Peace is the dream of It'll Do Lane. Peace is the reality of God's Immeasurably More.

Read Ephesians 2:14-16.

Complete the following sentence. *"For he himself is our ____________________, ..."*

What has He created *"in place of the two"*?

What has He broken down and abolished?

What does He want to create in Himself?

What is He reconciling?

What is the result of reconciliation?

Humbling, isn't it? The thing our souls thirst for the most deeply is found in the sweet waters of His presence. The ache that causes our hearts to toss and turn at night is soothed by the reality of His love. Peace. He Himself is our peace. He doesn't give us peace. He doesn't direct us toward peace. He doesn't lay out a plan for peace. Peace isn't a product you package, something you sell, or directions to be followed. Peace is a Person you embrace.

The peace that He offers you was purchased on the cross. It did not come cheap or easy, but it is free to your heart.

In order to give you peace within Himself, He had to use His flesh to break down and destroy a wall. It was a wall of hostility. A wall that separated you from God. A wall that divided you from your neighbor. A wall that created mistrust and suspicion. You built that wall with your sin. Thick and high, it rose out of the dust of your dreams as layer after layer of broken commandments, neglected regulations, and ignored ordinances piled up to testify against you. He used His body to silence the evidence against you. He absorbed the penalty due for not living out the holiness to which the Law directs our hearts. Now out of the broken rubble of your rebellion, He seeks to build something new.

Immeasurably More

Read Genesis 4:1-8. How did sin create an environment of hostility between men?

When sin entered the world, it did more than devastate our relationship with God. It damaged our relationships with each other as well. We misunderstood a fundamental truth about our hearts. Our connection to each other mirrors our connection to God. A strong and healthy connection to the heart of God allows us to have strong and healthy relationships with each other. When our connection with God falters, it impacts the way we relate to each other.

Where do you most clearly see the connection between the health of your relationship with God and the condition of your relationships with others?

Through His bridge-building, peace-making work on the cross, Jesus seeks to create one new man in the place of two. He seeks to make enemies friends, strangers family, aliens citizens, and those who are separated united. Peace with God means that we can live in peace with each other. As He binds us together in His blood, He reconciles us to God. All of us become connected as one body, one family, one household, and one people.

Write Isaiah 32:18.

Here is the promise of the Immeasurably More life. Destroying hostility and breaking down walls that separate us from God and each other is the first step out of It'll Do Lane. But He wants to build something in your life as well. He wants to house your heart in His presence. He longs for you to make your home in His peace. He wants His secure walls to be your dwelling place. He used the nails and beams of a cross to create a quiet resting place for your soul.

It'll Do Lane

My heart is a wrestling mat. I am constantly wrestling with shame, guilt, doubt, and fear. It gnaws at me, grabbing hold of me at the oddest times. My relationships with others seem out of sync. There is a disquiet that seems to permeate my connections with others. We are all just making it through the world the best we can. It'll have to do.

Immeasurably More

Peace saturates my soul. It defines my relationship with God and infuses itself into my connections to others. Peace doesn't mean there is never conflict. It means that Christ is working in me to demolish the things that create conflict within me, while building and creating pathways to unity, harmony, and reconciliation for me to walk.

Choosing a Home For Your Heart

Peace doesn't change your circumstances. It changes your perspective. You might still live in the same house, be surrounded by the same people, have the same amount of money in the bank, and be faced with the same challenges. Living in His peace means having the confidence to see those circumstances as pathways into His presence rather than walls that stop us in our tracks. Examine a situation in your life in which you would like to experience more peace. Make a list of the impact that deliberately living in His peace might have on the situation. Let Philippians 4:6-7 help you make the move.

Day 3

When you are building a house, it is important to include doorways. Doorways provide access. They are the entry points into your home and your life. A house with no doors would make no sense in our world. Of course, we put locks on our doors. The real test of accessibility is found in who holds the keys. They are the people who are closest to our hearts, the ones we trust with who we are, and the hearts that are most closely linked to our own.

Read Ephesians 2:17-18.

What did Jesus come and preach?

To whom did He preach this message?

What do we have through Him?

Peace is about more than destroying walls of hostility and building bridges of connection. It is also about opening doors. Jesus came with a specific and special message. It is a gospel of peace. Good news about the access we can have to the Father through the blood and sacrifice of Jesus.

Access is a big deal in our society. It is a measure of fame, power, money, and status. The more of a celebrity someone is, the more restricted the access to that person. Someone with an open door policy promotes access. Someone who lives with their door closed invites privacy and limits interaction.

No matter our station in life, we all deal in a complex balance of access. Strangers on the street and the clerk at the store have a limited amount of access to our lives. Friends and acquaintances have a bit more access. Our closest friends and family have the deepest access into our lives. Marriage, by its nature, is a covenant of access. We commit ourselves to giving the person we marry the most intimate access to our lives and hearts. To protect the integrity of that relationship, we promise that no matter with whom else we share other parts of our lives, there will be certain pieces of our hearts that we will only share with our spouse. They will be the only ones with access.

Write John 10:7.

Here is the good news of Jesus' preaching. He is the door. His very body creates the access point we need to enter into the presence of the Father. By His Spirit, we have entry. By His blood, we have a relationship that connects us to God. By the cross, He destroys the obstacles that get in the way. By His risen, resurrected life, we have the ability and opportunity to move freely within the heart of God.

The other exciting part of this good news is that access isn't limited to just a few. He sends the message out to those who are far away and those who are nearby. Everyone can come through the door of Christ. Anyone with a heart surrendered to His love can enter and find a place. Access isn't dependent on who you are, but on Who you know.

Read Genesis 3:8, 22-24. What access did Adam and Eve forfeit when they chose to settle for less than God's best?

One of the devastating consequences of Adam and Eve's choice in the Garden was that they could no longer live in the intimate presence of God. No more walking with Him in the cool of the evening, no more heart-to-heart moments of unblemished connection. Instead, they had to leave the Garden of Eden. They no longer had the same kind of access to His presence that they had once shared.

But it is important to see a singular truth. Before God limited their access to the Garden of Eden, they limited God's access to their hearts. When they hid from God, they were attempting to block His access to their lives. They didn't want God to see. They didn't want to let God in. And that's the way it works on It'll Do Lane.

There are really two doors. Jesus is the door into the presence of God. But you have a door as well. A door into your heart. Only you get to decide whether to allow God access into your life.

Read Revelation 3:20.

What is Jesus doing?

What promise does He make to those who open the door and give Him access?

Access flows both ways. Jesus opens the door into the peace of the Father. He makes that accessible to anyone who comes to Him in obedience, surrender, humility, and repentance. But access is a two-way street. In order to obtain the access Jesus offers, we have to provide Him with access to our lives. We must commit to a relationship where we walk in each other's hearts.

Immeasurably More

Living on It'll Do Lane has nothing to do with not having access to Jesus. That is available to everyone. Living on It'll Do Lane is about not giving Jesus access to our hearts. We close off places in our lives, telling Him they are off-limits. We want to hold onto secrets, put up "private property" signs, and tell Him that certain things belong only to us.

The way into God's Immeasurably More is simply to open the door. Open the door of your heart. Give Him access. Sometimes we fear that Jesus will be scared off by what He sees behind our doors. Remember Adam and Eve? God knew what they were trying to hide. He wasn't shocked, just sad that they closed their hearts to Him. The peace that comes with God's Immeasurably More is that Christ is prepared to deal with the mess that comes with our doors. He has the power. He gives us the grace. He offers His love. His door is open for you. Where you live depends on whether or not you will open your door for Him.

Day 4

Home is a special place. Home is where we feel most comfortable. It is where we let our guard down, open up our hearts, and live our most real lives. Home sees us when we aren't at our best, when we struggle, and when we don't know where else to go. Home is the place where we celebrate our victories, share our joys, and reveal what truly touches our hearts.

Read Ephesians 2:19-22.

How does Jesus change your identity?

On what is the household of God built?

Describe how the whole building is coming together in Him.

For whom are you becoming a dwelling place?

We tend to live our lives as islands, especially on It'll Do Lane. We keep to ourselves, waving at neighbors across the fence, and expecting to live self-sufficient, "don't really need anybody" kind of lives. We can be pleasant and friendly, but then we close our doors, relish our personal space, and do what we want to do. We live as strangers in familiar places.

When we move into God's Immeasurably More, we shed the island life and join a community. It is a life in which we are connected to God and interconnected with each other. We live in each other's lives, walk in each other's hearts, carry each other's burdens, and share each other's joys.

This passage describes four ways in which we are connected to each other through Jesus.

Connected in Identity. Leaving It'll Do Lane behind means shedding our identity as loners. We are no longer strangers and aliens. We now belong. We fit. We are connected. We are fellow citizens with others who live within the kingdom of God. We unite with others who live lives of consecration and commitment to the King.

We become saints. We shed the label of sinner, and take on the identity of one who walks with God. We struggle with sin, but it no longer defines us. We are no longer in sin because we are in Him.

Living in God's Immeasurably More means that we live as members of the household of God. We are part of a family. Connected because of the blood of Jesus, we now share a heart, a hope, and a home with others who belong to the Father.

How does understanding our identity connection help us live in God's Immeasurably More?

Connected by Roots. Shaping this new identity in our lives, God plants His family on solid ground, giving us deep roots and a strong base. He builds His household on the foundation of the apostles and prophets. Their words have rung with the message of life for centuries. They point the way to God, call people to walk in His ways, hold up truth, provide strength for the journey, and offer light in the darkness. Each word spoken by the apostles and prophets points to the same place. They all point to Jesus. When we build our lives on the Word of God, we build our lives on Jesus.

Not only is Jesus the foundation of our heart's home, He is the chief cornerstone. He is the standard and the anchor for every part of our lives. Everything is measured through Him. Everything flows from Him. Everything is centered around Him.

How does being rooted together in Christ help us live the Immeasurably More life?

Connected in Purpose. As Jesus works in our lives, joining us together heart by heart, we are growing into a holy temple in the Lord. His purpose is taking shape in our lives. Worship, praise, service, and reverence flow from lives connected in Him. The church stands as a priesthood dedicated to living in awareness of God's glory and goodness. It is commissioned with a message to share, a love to declare, and a grace to proclaim. Holiness permeates our lives as the image of the Savior takes shape in our hearts.

How does being connected in purpose help us move into God's Immeasurably More?

Connected in Peace. You are not a nameless brick in a massive structure. This is personal. What God is building, He is building in your life. God is building within you a dwelling place for His heart. He wants to live with you, abide with you, move in and make a home with you.

Write John 14:23.

This is where He connects our hearts to His peace. Peace flows from living life in the presence of God. Peace is not defined by our circumstances. It doesn't depend on everything being just so, having all the answers, or getting it all together. Peace is defined by our connection to God, regardless of our circumstances. It doesn't matter if the sea is calm; it matters who you have in the boat.

It'll Do Lane

Personal and private are big words with me. There are just certain things that I am going to hang onto as my own. I will take care of my business. Being connected to others is sticky, and requires me to share more than I am comfortable doing. They might criticize me or want me to change. I feel like I am out here by myself, but it will have to do.

Immeasurably More

God calls me to open the door of my heart to His presence, His power, and His peace. When I let Him in, He moves me into a family, connects me with His purpose, and fills me with His peace. He is building something in me that is bigger, sturdier, and more satisfying than I could have ever asked or imagined for myself.

Choosing a Home For Your Heart

Home is where the heart is. Walk around the rooms of your heart. Where do you see evidence of God's peace and God's presence? Where do you see closed doors, places you have yet to let Him enter?

Immeasurable Purpose
Lesson 7

The sign in the classroom said, "If you aim at nothing, you will hit it." It's a great sign. It captures a truth that we live out every day. We were made for a purpose. We were made to live out a purpose. We were never meant to live aimless, purposeless, wandering-in-circles lives. Purpose gives shape to our days, sharpens our focus, and sets our direction. It embeds life with deep meaning and helps us make sense of our circumstances.

It'll Do Lane is populated with people who are living aimless lives. Walking without purpose is one of the most soul-defeating things in life. It robs us of a vitality that is meant to inspire us to dream, depend, and take dramatic steps of faith. The world will offer you a panorama of purposes that challenge you to invest your life in something less than the grand purpose God has in mind for you. The move into God's Immeasurably More means embracing God's purpose for your life. It means being deliberate about walking with called, consecrated, committed hearts. God has a purpose for you – a big, amazing, immeasurable purpose.

Day 1

Paul is a man who lives with purpose. He knows where he is going, who has called him, and what he is going to do each day. His single-mindedness is one of the things that we admire about him. Understanding your purpose provides a clarity we long for. It helps us set our priorities, and sort through the myriad of choices that come our way every day. This kind of purpose is not just for apostles and "special" people. It is for you, and you can begin to live out that purpose today, right where you are.

Read Ephesians 3:1-3.

Immeasurably More

How does Paul describe himself?

What was given to Paul?

What was made known to Paul?

Arrested in Jerusalem, Paul now sits awaiting trial before Caesar in Rome. While there, he uses the time to write letters to Christians, encouraging them to live out the purpose and understand the plan that God has for them. It is not a purpose that is limited to a specific time, place, or person. It is an eternal purpose that God is working out in the heart of every person who chooses to live in His Immeasurably More.

Read Romans 8:28-29. What is God's purpose for those that love Him?

This is an amazing passage of promise and purpose. God is at work in your life. Today. Right now. He is actively moving to draw you deeper into His ultimate purpose for your heart. He is at work in all things. That little *all* is a big word. Don't skip over it. It says that God stands with you in every circumstance, every ordinary, regular piece of your day in order to unleash His eternal, bigger-than-you-can-imagine purpose in you. Sometimes we think that purpose is only played out on a big stage while doing special, applause-worthy kinds of things. "All things" means while you are doing the laundry, going to the bank, and taking care of your kids. It means what you do when you are dressed up and having a good hair day, as well as the things you do when you are in your comfortable clothes with no make-up on.

In all things, in every moment, God is working for our good. He stands in every experience, every opportunity, and every situation orchestrating His great and glorious purpose in our lives. This does not mean that God causes everything to happen or that every circumstance or challenge that enters your life is His will. It does mean that He is working in each one of those moments to bring about His greatest good for your life.

Determined and set from before the beginning of time, His plan is for you to be conformed to the image of His Son. He wants you to look like Jesus.

What does it mean to look like Jesus?

We all long to catch of glimpse of how our small lives fit into the big picture. We want to make a difference, leave a legacy, and to add our note to the chorus of praise that fills heaven.

Looking like Jesus, walking in His steps, mirroring His heart, and imitating His character is the way God calls us into His purpose and works out His will in our lives.

This is the purpose for which you are called to be a steward. We are administrators of God's grace, ambassadors of His message, and agents of His will. He has given us a purpose to live out and a life in which to live it out. Neither the purpose nor the life are our own. They belong to Him. He works in us and through us, continually using our surrender to shape us more completely into the image of Jesus. Even in our stubbornness, He is moving to draw us into a deeper reflection of His Son.

The It'll Do life says that it all belongs to me. I can do with my life what I want. The truth is that what I want is not very grand. It is limited to what I can see, do, or imagine. When I walk in my own self-designed purpose, it ends with me feeling a bit hollow and asking, "Is this all there is?"

Write I Corinthians 2:2.

This is Paul's statement of purpose. He resolves to know nothing but Jesus Christ and Him crucified. He determines to fill every moment with Jesus. It doesn't matter what he is doing, who he is with, where he is going, or what kind of day he is having – Jesus is going to permeate everything. He is going to let Christ's holiness, love, grace, joy, focus, and wisdom influence and shape every action, thought, motive, and interaction.

In opening his life for the image of Christ to take shape in him, Paul understands that God will use that surrender to touch lives, call hearts, proclaim a message, and bring glory to His name. The same is true for you. When you commit to living out God's purpose in your life – looking like Jesus – God will use your surrender in ways you cannot even begin to imagine.

Looking like Jesus is God's purpose for your life. He has entrusted you with His grace. Living out this purpose doesn't require special training, special timing, or special talent. It requires a humble heart and a surrendered spirit. You can start living in the fullness of God's immeasurable purpose right now. Resolve to look like Jesus. Then, go do it.

What are three specific ways in which you can look like Jesus today?

Day 2

God's purpose for your life is not a secret or a mystery. He revealed His immeasurable purpose for your life in the person of Jesus. When Jesus walked on the earth, He showed us exactly how God wants us all to live in His Immeasurably More.

Read Ephesians 3:4-6.

When was the mystery of Christ made known?

What is the mystery that Christ is now revealing through Paul?

The fullness of the revelation of Jesus Christ was not completely understood until after Jesus' resurrection. There are hints of His coming, pictures of His ministry, and promises about His movement among men woven throughout the Old Testament. But the fullness of God's purpose through Jesus was a mystery until the Divine wrapped Himself in flesh and walked among us. Even during His life on earth, no one seemed to grasp the lengths to which He would go to bring us salvation. The power that would be unleashed, the love that would be displayed, the grace that would revealed did not come into full view until Jesus was done with His work.

We are blessed to stand on this side of that revelation. We know that everyone is invited into the promise and purpose of Christ. His blood stands ready to cleanse every heart that seeks renewal, refreshment, and regeneration. God does not measure us by the external measures of man. Your heritage, skin color, gender, station in life, IQ, hair style, occupation, and body type don't make you or define you in the eyes of God. Looking like Jesus is what counts.

Read I Samuel 16:7. How do we learn to embrace God's directive to Samuel?

As we all come together in Christ, Jesus pours out His grace making us all fellow heirs and members of one body. There is a unity and connection that is unique among those who wear His name. We all understand that we stand in relationship with God only because of the blood of Jesus. Humility and gratitude binds our hearts together as we lift one voice to sing His praises and glorify His name.

There is one other description of our place in the family of God that is important. We are *"partakers of the promise in Christ Jesus through the gospel"* (verse 6). We each have a share in the promises of God. The idea of partaking or sharing, however, is a very active picture and one that helps us understand what it means to live in God's Immeasurably More.

Define *partake*.

Partake is a participation word. It gives us an interesting and convicting insight into God's purpose for our lives. Have you ever watched small children at a swimming pool? There are generally two different pictures that play out at the pool. On one hand are the kids who are having a ball in the water. Splashing, dunking, and floating, they are wet. They are in the water, learning to enjoy all the pool has to offer as a place of refreshment and joy. Then there are the kids on the side of the pool. Can you see their faces? Generally, these are not happy faces. Hesitant, scared, stubborn, or wary, these little ones content themselves with putting a toe in the water. They settle for sitting on the sidelines. They don't want to get in the water. The move from where they are into the water is too big of a move to make.

How does having that picture of the pool help you understand how God wants you to live in His Immeasurably More?

Do you see why this word *partake* is so important? God calls us into the deep end of His purpose. He wants us to be soaked in His grace, drenched with His love, saturated with His vision, and immersed in His will. He wants us to be participators and partakers in this Immeasurably More life He offers us in Christ. He doesn't want us to be spectators or side-liners. When we sit on the side of the pool and settle for sticking our toe in the water, we have planted our heart right in the middle of It'll Do Lane.

Immeasurably More

You can't dabble at Christianity. There is no such thing as a part-time follower of Jesus. It isn't a life you can try on like a dress, discarding it if you think it doesn't fit well enough. You can't take on Christlikeness only when it is convenient, when it doesn't interfere with other plans, or when you need a bit of comfort. You are either in the pool or you're not. Your ability to swim is not what matters. God will teach you to swim. What matters is your willingness to get in the water.

On a scale of 1 – 10, prayerfully consider how much of a partaker you are in the Immeasurably More life. A "1" means that you are sitting securely by the side of the pool. A "10" means that you are diving deeply into His Immeasurably More.

What will you commit to doing this week to more fully participate in the life Jesus wants you to live?

It'll Do Lane

I am still trying to figure out my purpose. Right now it is all I can do to make it through my day. I do the Christian thing when I can. Between work, family, and trying to enjoy life, there isn't much time. I know I should be doing more, but for now, it will have to do.

Immeasurably More

God is working His purpose in my life. It is an amazing thing to think that He is shaping me to look like Jesus, but He is. Holding something back isn't an option any more. The deeper I go, the more He fills me with Himself, the more aware I am of His grace, and the more He forms His purpose in me.

Choosing a Home For Your Heart

Write "My purpose is to look like Jesus" on an index card. Carry it with you, post it on your bathroom mirror, and stick it on your refrigerator. How will you let His purpose permeate your family? Your work? The way you walk through the store? How you use your time? What you watch on television? How you relate to your neighbors?

Day 3

So what shape does this purpose take in our lives? We are all called to look like Jesus. God has put you here at this time and in this place because there are people here who need to see Jesus in you. I am not going to be able to walk into your home or your office and look like Jesus for the people there. Only you can do that. There are people I meet that you will never see. It is my purpose to look like Jesus for them. Wherever you walk today, whatever circumstances you find yourself in, God is working in you to reveal Jesus to the world.

Read Ephesians 3:7-10.

How does Paul describe himself?

How does Paul evaluate his own ability to carry out God's purpose?

What three things will be revealed as Paul lives out the purpose to which God has called him?

Paul describes himself as a minister and servant of the gospel. While understanding that Paul was given a very specific task as an apostle, it is important to see that we are called to the same purpose. The same Spirit that dwelt in Paul dwells in you today. The same power that transformed Paul is transforming you. The same Immeasurably More life that Paul lived is the life God wants you to live.

In what way are you a servant of the gospel?

Living in God's immeasurable purpose means understanding that we are servants in His kingdom. Like Paul, we can stand in amazement that God would use us at all. But He does. It is part of His purpose to use His people for His glory. We are servants according to the gift of God's grace and by the working of His power in our lives. We have been taken into His care and empowered to serve Him.

Immeasurably More

It'll Do Lane residents aren't servants. They are more like independent contractors. Independent contractors hold control over where and when they work. They get to decide which jobs they will take. They hold responsibility for making their own way and paying their own expenses. A servant lives in the bounty of the King. An independent contractor stands alone.

How does keeping a clear vision of how deeply grace changes our lives help us avoid the independent contractor mindset?

Learning to live in God's immeasurable purpose takes a very specific shape and has a very specific impact in our lives. The shape of our purpose is Jesus. Everything about our lives must be in conformity with His nature and character.

We are called to live cross-shaped, cross-empowered, cross-centered, cross-defining, cross-proclaiming lives.

The impact of living such a life is three-fold. Looking like Jesus will leave a taste of Christ in others as they hear, see, and experience the purpose of God being worked out in our lives.

Hear. Paul is called specifically to preach to the Gentiles the unsearchable riches of Christ. In the same way, the people around you will hear the name of Jesus through you as you walk in His purpose. Your changed, transformed, new life testifies to the unsearchable riches of His grace. Every step you take in His will echoes with His immeasurable power and deep love. As your attitude takes on the shape of Jesus, it will be evident in your words, choices, motives, and interactions. Your life will become a marker that points others to the cross.

How will looking like Jesus change the way you hear? How will it change the way that others hear Jesus in your life?

See. In God's work of salvation and redemption, Paul is commissioned with bringing to light the plan of Christ and including the Gentiles. All Christians are called to bring light to the world. When we commit ourselves to Jesus, He makes a fundamental shift in our nature. Once we were darkness. Now we are light. Looking like Jesus means letting that light shine. When we let our lights shine, others can see the plan of God because they can see Jesus in us. Our light serves as an invitation to everyone who sees it to leave the darkness of It'll Do Lane and walk in the brightness of His Immeasurably More.

Read Matthew 5:14-16. In what way are you deliberate about letting your light shine?

Experience. God wants to use the church to make something amazing known to the world. In you, the manifold wisdom of God is being revealed. It is as big of a deal as it sounds like it is. Connected to the Christians from every people, tribe, language, and nation, you help others to experience the many-folded wisdom of God. God uses each of us as a canvas for His grace. Your heart is like a piece of a quilt. Alone, we each have certain beauty and our own unique color and texture. Pieced together by His love and grace, we have the power to take the world's breath away.

Think of three friends who look like Jesus. How do each of them show you a different fold or facet of God's wisdom and grace?

Day 4

An important component of the Immeasurably More life God offers us is to live in His immeasurable purpose. We all long for a deep purpose to guide our days, value our time, and shape our vision. We get stuck on It'll Do Lane when we invest our hearts in things that are less than God's best for us. We step into God's Immeasurably More when we embrace His desire for us to look like Jesus. He calls us to dive into the deep end of His grace as we become partakers in His purpose, and as He shows the impact that living in His purpose will have on the world.

Read Ephesians 3:11-13.

Describe the longevity of our purpose in Christ.

What three things do we have because of our faith in Jesus?

How does an understanding of his purpose help Paul reassure those worried about his imprisonment?

Having a purpose changes the way you walk. It sets the order of my day. It helps me evaluate the opportunities that come my way. It infuses value into my actions and lets me see my life from a different perspective. When you understand your purpose, everything becomes clearer.

As Paul finishes describing this aspect of the Immeasurably More life, he reveals one more characteristic of the immeasurable purpose in which we are called to live. It is eternal. Everything else we can invest our hearts in is temporary, no matter how good it is. Spouses die, children grow up, jobs end, pleasure is fleeting, money runs out, and beauty fades. Looking like Jesus is the only thing that will extend into eternity.

Read I John 3:2. What will happen when He appears?

The bigger our purpose, the greater its ability to energize our souls, lift our vision, help us overcome our obstacles, answer our critics, and direct our steps. An eternal purpose given to us by an Almighty God to live in the image of Jesus certainly fits the bill.

Walking in this purpose unleashes the Immeasurably More life for our souls. On It'll Do Lane, we walk for ourselves. Our purpose is limited to our vision, our power, and our know-how. We can come up with some good things to do, but none measures up to the immeasurable purpose God has for us in Jesus.

Paul has outlined how God's immeasurable purpose will impact the world as it hears, sees, and experiences the way Jesus is honored in your life. Now he tells us the impact that living in that purpose will have in you – boldness, confidence and access.

What does it mean to live boldly?

What does it mean to live confidently?

Why is access in Christ important to having both boldness and confidence?

Boldness. When we walk in faith in God's immeasurable purpose, we can walk with boldness. Boldness is best seen in what we do. When we are bold, we are able to take the next step. We don't hesitate to walk in faith, even if our sight is limited. There is an adventurous, imaginative quality to boldness that inspires others to join in. There is also an aspect of being bold that speaks to being distinctive and willing to stand out.

Boldness is the quality that pushes us out of our comfort zones and challenges us to walk deeper in faith, stronger in grace, and further into His Immeasurably More.

Do you have bold faith? How do we develop bolder faith?

How does Psalm 138:1-3 outline a process for developing bolder faith?

Immeasurably More

Confidence. Confidence flows into the heart of the one who deliberately determines to live in God's immeasurable purpose. Where boldness best defines our actions, confidence speaks to the heart. Confidence rests in the assurance of what we know to be true. It speaks to our perspective and the way in which we react to the world around us. Confidence rids our hearts of the unsure, aimless steps that often consume us. In Him, we have confidence about where we are going, the purpose He has for our lives, and the standard by which He wants us to live.

Do you have confident faith? How do we grow a more confident faith?

How does Jeremiah 17:7-9 teach us to grow a more confident faith?

Access. We can have boldness and confidence because Jesus gives us access to the Father. Without this access, we would be on our own. Through Jesus, we have the ability to enter into the throne room of heaven and stand in the presence of the King. Our boldness and confidence flow from Who we know. Because God is on our side, we can take new steps of faith. Worship and gratitude keep our eyes fixed on Him and help stretch our vision of who He is and where He wants to take us. Planting ourselves in His presence gives our hearts the deep roots we need to fuel our confidence.

Write Hebrews 4:16.

It'll Do Lane

I want to make a difference. I really do, but it is hard to change the world by yourself. My ordinary life isn't really going to make a difference for anybody. I'll just try to be a good person and hope it is enough.

Immeasurably More

Living in God's immeasurable purpose allows me to walk in boldness and have deep confidence because of the access I have through Jesus. I am excited about the life God calls me to live. I know that looking like Jesus has a greater impact than I can ask for or imagine because He is using me for His eternal purpose.

Choosing a Home For Your Heart

Fixing your **AIM** is important if you want to live in God's immeasurable purpose.

A - Answer God's call to purpose. Ask Him to help you embrace the purpose He has for you in Christ.

I – Invest your heart in living out His purpose. Let go of the "smaller" purposes that consume our time and attention. Dedicate your heart to filling every moment with Jesus.

M – Move in His direction. Don't just make plans. Take a step of faith. Be bold.

Immeasurable Faith
Lesson 8

Faith is the substance of victory. *"For everyone who has been born of God overcomes the world. And this is the victory that has overcome the world – our faith. Who is it that overcomes the world except the one who believes that Jesus is the Son of God?"* – I John 5:4-5.

The Immeasurably More life is a life of victory. It allows us to overcome fear, stagnation, doubt, anxiety, and aimlessness. Christ's victory over sin opens the door for us to live in the full intensity of His grace. Faith in the One who has overcome the world is the key to leaving the emptiness of It'll Do Lane and taking up residence in the delight of His presence. It expands hope, clarifies vision, empowers surrender, and aligns priorities. Faith is essential to living in God's Immeasurably More. Faith allows us to see the possibilities of stepping out of what we imagine for ourselves into the vision God has for our hearts.

Day 1

The picture of the Immeasurably More life is taking shape. In Ephesians, God offers us an amazing view of what it means to make our home in His heart. He is willing to pour love, power, grace, peace, and purpose into our lives as He invites us to abide completely in Him. Immeasurable faith is the final component of this Immeasurably More life that He wants to give us.

Read Ephesians 3:14-16.

To whom does Paul bow his knees?

By what measure does he ask that we be granted strength?

From where does this strength flow? To where does it flow?

As Paul draws together the picture of the Immeasurably More life, he kneels once again in prayer. This is an essential element of living in God's Immeasurably More. Paul flows back and forth between talking to us and talking to God. He understands that God is in the middle of every conversation, that He empowers every step, and that His presence and participation in every piece of our lives is critical if we are going to live Immeasurably More lives.

Immeasurable faith begins with a constant awareness of God's presence. He is here, right now, very close to you. He promises to never leave or forsake you. His presence in your life is not a question. Whether or not you have the eyes and heart to see Him is the substance of faith. It'll Do Lane faith expects God to show up on Sundays and to be there in emergencies. Immeasurably More faith lives in the reality of God's constant presence.

How do we develop eyes that are open to His presence in every moment of our lives?

The process of developing these eyes of faith is really quite simple. We have to ask to see Him, expect to see Him, and practice seeing Him.

Ask to see Him – God wants you to be aware of His presence. Ask Him to help you have eyes open to His presence.

Expect to see Him – Our expectations often determine our realities. Believe that He is working in your day. Trust that He wants you to find Him. Depend on His faithfulness and rely on His promises.

Practice seeing Him – It takes practice to see the hand of God on your life. Walk with someone who recognizes Him easily. Count your blessings. Pay attention to the small joys.

How would you explain faith to someone who does not know God?

Faith is a move of the heart that is rooted in the character of God. Faith begins in the hands of God. He always moves first. As He opens His heart and moves on our behalves, He calls us to connect with Him and walk in relationship with Him. God creates a world and invites Adam and Eve to live with Him. God prepares a home, and calls Abraham to walk with Him. God opens a path through the sea, and bids Israel to move under the canopy of His protection and victory.

Every time God reveals His heart, He invites us to respond by moving our hearts a little closer to His.

Paul's movement in these verses outlines a path for our faith.

Faith starts with surrender. *"For this reason I bow my knees..."* Faith always finds its roots in the character of God. Surrender acknowledges that God is sovereign, that He is in control, and that our best move is to put our hearts in His hands.

Faith is grounded in relationship. *"...before the Father, from whom every family in heaven and on earth is named,..."* Faith is not a theoretical exercise of the mind. It is a relationship, a friendship, a communion, and a connection. Like any relationship, it is built on time, trust, and transparency.

Faith is fueled by His glory. *"...that according to the riches of his glory..."* This is where our definition of faith most often goes off course. We think that faith is up to us. We view God as the recipient of our faith, rather than the active resource for our faith. My faith cannot be sustained by my own strength. It order to grow and thrive, it must be fueled by the depths of His love and the riches of His glory.

Faith is empowered by His presence. *"...he may grant you to be strengthened with power through his Spirit in your inner being."* Jesus knocks. We open the door. God moves in. What God touches, He transforms. That is the cycle of faith. Jesus knocks on the door of my pride. I let Him in. His Spirit moves in, and begins to shape me into the image of Jesus. Now He knocks on the door of my selfishness. I let Him in, and the transformation continues.

How will these four steps help you move from It'll Do Lane faith into God's Immeasurably More?

Day 2

Transformation is at the heart of God's great desire for you. It breaks His heart to see you trapped on It'll Do Lane. When we settle for something less than His presence, He sees more clearly than we do all that we are giving up. Living on It'll Do Lane denies our souls the full flight that they are meant to take. Instead of stretching, growing, expanding, and thriving, we shrivel, shrink, and collapse.

The faith in which He wants us to live proclaims His abundance, and is life-giving and soul-enhancing. In faith, we stay connected to Him. Within that connection, He nourishes our hearts, feeds our souls, strengthens our spirits, and delights us with His nearness. Faith is the glue that binds us to His heart.

Read Ephesians 3:17-19.

What opens the door for Christ to dwell in our hearts?

In what way does Paul pray we are connected to love?

What does Paul pray that we comprehend?

How full does Paul pray our lives will be in Christ?

Transformation is necessary if we are going to live in God's Immeasurably More. Released from sin and freed from the guilt and shame that comes with walking in our own ways, our souls need to be recalibrated, refurbished, and renewed. Living on It'll Do Lane causes them to dry up and wither.

Stretching our souls, then, becomes one of the goals of God's transformation. He wants us to see farther, dream bigger, and walk deeper into His love. Faith might be best expressed in our willingness to be stretched, to hold more of God within us, and to be full of the fullness of God rather than the hot air of this world.

Pouring out his heart in prayer, this is exactly what Paul prays for – elastic, stretchy faith. Faith that can expand to hold all of the goodness, abundance, richness, and overwhelming beauty of His heart. He prays that this transformation takes shape in four different ways in your life.

Dwell. The first and most important way in which immeasurable faith stretches us is found in the way that it makes room for Christ to dwell in our hearts. Living in God's Immeasurably More is not as much about where we choose to live as it is about how we make room for Christ to live in us. On It'll Do Lane, we settle for being neighbors with Jesus. He lives in the area. We wave, share a fence, and talk on the driveway. But we don't let Him into where we really live.

In the Immeasurably More life, Jesus buys our house and moves in, inviting us to live with Him. He immediately begins to remodel, throwing out anything that doesn't match His character. He then brings in all the things that showcase His mercy and magnify His grace in our lives. His desire is to move room by room through our hearts, creating a place of beauty and love that welcomes His presence.

Read Psalm 37. Make two columns, noting the blessings that belong to those who choose to dwell in God and the reality of life on It'll Do Lane.

Grounded. Another impact of His gracious transformation on our hearts is that it roots our faith in His immeasurable love. We live on a firm foundation. We are grounded in the unmovable, unshakable, unwavering love of God Himself. Life on It'll Do Lane is a constant balancing act. We are always trying to keep our footing, picking up the pieces when circumstances shift. Rooted and grounded in Jesus means that we can stand confidently in every situation. We are not going to move because He is not going to move.

Read Matthew 13:5, 20-21. What happens when we aren't rooted and grounded in Christ?

Comprehend. One of the most beautiful stretching moments happens when we are able to comprehend the vastness of God's love for us. Comprehend is an interesting word. It means more than just to know or even understand. It is a picture of seizing, embracing, grasping, and uniting. When we comprehend His love, we take it into ourselves. It becomes part of us. We catch hold of it and hang on for dear life. Paul prays that no matter where we look – up, down, near, or far – we will grab onto Jesus' love. His love is our greatest, truest reality. When we can comprehend that, it helps us make sense of everything else.

Read I John 4:7-12. How does God help our hearts comprehend what love really is?

Full. Here is where we experience the abundance of having immeasurable faith. We are full, filled with the fullness of God. When we live in His Immeasurably More, the ache of emptiness fades. The raw places in our souls receive the soothing balm of His grace. Our restlessness is overwhelmed by His peace. Our weariness is lifted by His strength. Our loneliness is answered by His presence. Our wandering is given direction by His purpose, and the worthlessness that eats away at our hearts is overcome by His love.

The beautiful truth is that this fullness is ever expanding. The more our faith stretches, the more of God that is available to us. He is unlimited, without end, and everlasting. Exploring the depths of His fullness is the adventure that will not only take a lifetime, but an eternity.

Read John 1:16. What flows out of His fullness into our lives?

It'll Do Lane

Faith is a good thing. I pull it out when I need a little comfort or need to reset the guilt meter. I don't know if it really makes a difference in my regular, ordinary day. It's nice to have in the hospital and at funerals. I probably need to work on my faith, but for now, it will have to do.

Immeasurably More

Faith opens my heart so that God can move in and work on me. It grounds me, sustains me, stretches me, and empowers me. Faith is the avenue through which God transforms me and fills me with Himself.

Choosing a Home For Your Heart

Spend some time talking to God about your faith. Ask Him to help you examine your faith, and give you a vision for the immeasurable faith He wants you to have. Remember, faith is best grounded in opening yourself up to how God wants to work in you. Ask for eyes to see Him, and a heart that is quick to respond to His presence.

Day 3

How big can you dream? Our dreams help us imagine beyond the moment. They give rise to hope, allow us to see a future different than our present reality, and inspire us to move toward something new. Our dreams not only have the power to shape our tomorrows, but also have substance today. They help us choose where to walk, how to live, what to do, and who to love.

Read Ephesians 3:20-21.

How does Paul describe God?

Where is His power at work?

Where does Paul pray God's glory will be?

Here is where living in God's Immeasurably More is leading us. As God works in our lives, transforming us, empowering us, and filling us with Himself, He pushes back the boundaries of what we think is possible.

Too many times our potential is limited by our vision. The size of our dreams matches the size of our strength. Our boundaries are defined by what we can do, or more likely, what we can't do. We settle for dreams that can live comfortably in our reality and that don't stretch our souls, or challenge our imaginations.

Define *immeasurably*.

How does this definition help you get a glimpse of what God wants to do in your life?

The Immeasurably More into which God calls us is not a pipe dream or a flight of fancy. It is grounded in the truth of His character. He is able. In order to live out God-sized dreams, we have to be absolutely certain that He is big enough, strong enough, faithful enough, and loving enough to make those dreams a reality in our lives.

God loves to delight us. The Bible is filled with moments in which man says "impossible" and God reveals His "more than you can ask or imagine" solution. Just ask Sarah – ninety birthday candles and a baby shower all in the same year. Watch Joseph wave the signet ring of Pharaoh as he drives past the prison in which he was once held. Stand with the Israelites by the Red Sea. Walk onto the battlefield with David and Goliath. Go up onto the mountain with Elijah. Spend the day talking to Hezekiah and Esther. Visit a little village in Galilee called Nazareth. Step outside the gates of Jerusalem and turn your eyes to Golgotha.

Write Matthew 19:26.

God has not stopped doing the impossible. He only asks that we open up our hearts to the possibility that He can work in us in ways beyond our own imaginations. He doesn't want us to limit His power by our strength, His dreams by our boundaries, His riches by our resources, or His wisdom by our knowledge.

The Immeasurably More life means being willing to step beyond what we can ask or imagine, and make room in our lives for God to unleash His vision in us.

We are not necessarily talking about doing grand things on a big stage. God wants to release His Immeasurably More into your life right where you are in this moment. "But I am just a ....." Don't limit God's ability to work in you and through you. He has the power to touch lives, open eyes, calm fears, dry tears, forgive sins, and transform hearts in your house, your neighborhood, your job, and your church. And He might just use you to do it. He might call you to pray, to give a hug, to write a card, to change a diaper, to speak a kind word, to extend an invitation, to call a friend, or to walk with someone. Don't underestimate the power that God can bring into what we see as ordinary moments. God has the ability to touch this minute with eternity, to plant seeds for glory in the things we view as regular or mundane.

Let God fire your imagination for a minute. How might an ordinary moment in your day look if it was infused with God's Immeasurably More?

And that is the point. When we live in God's Immeasurably More, nothing is ordinary anymore. Because we understand that everything is touched by our extraordinary God, every part of our lives takes on a dimension, a richness, and a purpose that is deeper and more meaningful than we can imagine. Our todays are tied to forever. Our actions spotlight His glory. Our lives become showcases for His power. Our hearts become a picture of Jesus for the world.

So what will it be? You can settle for living a life that stretches only as far as your own imagination. Build a little house on It'll Do Lane, and get comfortable. That is as far as you will ever go. Or you can take a step of faith into God's Immeasurably More. Let Him define your dreams, map out your possibilities, and stretch your vision. He is able to do it. He has the power to do it. All He needs is the key to your heart.

Day 4

We have reached the heart of Paul's letter. Walking through the first three chapters of Ephesians gives us an amazing picture of the Immeasurably More life God wants for us. It is a life filled with His love, empowered by His might, and transformed by His grace. Walking with Jesus allows His peace to overwhelm our souls as we learn to live in His purpose. It is a life defined by His presence in our hearts.

As we wrap this section up, it is important to pause and pull the whole picture together. These glimpses into God's Immeasurably More have also pulled back the curtain on how our hearts tend to settle for so much less than God's best. We build houses on It'll Do Lane, letting the world convince us that this is as good as it gets. We let busyness take the place of purpose, allow control to override surrender, choose worry instead of peace, and settle for being neighbors rather than dwelling in the fullness of God's presence.

Walking one more time through Ephesians 3:14-21 gives us the opportunity to examine the amazing, abundant, rich, passionate life offered to us through the blood of Jesus.

Fill in the blanks to complete the Scripture passages.

3:14-15 - "For this reason I bow my knees before the ________________, from whom every family in heaven and on earth is named,"

At the center of the Immeasurably More life is an intimate, personal, close relationship with God. We live connected to His heart. Our souls can rest in the arms of a Father who delights in us and cherishes us beyond measure.

3:16 - "that according to the riches of his glory he may grant you to be ____________________with ____________________ through His Spirit in your ____________________ being."

The Immeasurably More life is one defined by His power. God moves in, strengthening us in our innermost being. It is a strength that flows into our hearts through the power of God and then overflows into every other aspect of our lives.

3:17a – "so that ________________ may ____________________ in your hearts through ____________________"

The presence of God in our hearts is the defining characteristic of the Immeasurably More life. His presence makes us whole. It transforms what is broken by sin, bruised by guilt, and smashed by shame, changing us into a residence for His glory. Faith is surrender in action. It opens the door to our hearts and lets Him in.

3:17b – "that you, being ______________________ and grounded in ____________________."

We live in a shaky world. The Immeasurably More life promises to root and ground us in the unshakeable, unmovable, unwavering love of God. He offers us a life of stability in the face of life's storms.

3:18-19a – "may have strength to ______________________ with all the saints what is the breadth and length and height and depth, and to know the ___________________ of _____________________ that ____________________ knowledge."

The Immeasurably More life transforms our vision and perspective. It helps us see through the fog of the world and catch a glimpse of how far the amazing, stunning love of Jesus stretches for us. It lets us live with confidence and certainty as we comprehend the immeasurable dimensions of His love.

3:19b – "that you may be ____________________ with all the ___________________ of ____________________."

Opening our hearts to the Immeasurably More of God floods our lives with a richness and abundance that we ache to embrace. Too often, we fill our lives with so much junk in an attempt to soothe the hunger for the fullness we can only experience in God.

3:20 – "Now to him who is ___________________ to do ____________________________ than all that we _______________ or _____________________, according to the _________________________ at work within us."

Lives filled with purpose. Hearts that have an impact far beyond our own imaginings. Dreams whose only boundaries are the will and goodness of God. Souls which live in the possibilities created by His power. Immeasurably More than we can ask or imagine.

Immeasurably More

3:21 – "to him be ____________________ in the church and in Christ Jesus throughout all generations, forever and ever. Amen."

The Immeasurably More life invites us to position our hearts for praise, live lives defined by worship, and have souls immersed in reverence and awe. We surrender our claim to the spotlight in order to bring Him glory and reflect His image to the world.

This is the life God offers you. It is an immeasurably bigger, richer, deeper, more passionate, purposeful, gracious life than we could ever imagine for ourselves. It is an invitation to make His love the address of your heart. But the choice is always yours. You can settle for It'll Do Lane, making yourself comfortable in the "good enough" of the world.

Complete the following chart by noting the It'll Do characteristic that is the opposite God's Immeasurably More.

God's Immeasurably More	It'll Do Lane
Intimate relationship with the Father	
Strengthened with power	
Dwelling in His presence	
Rooted and grounded in love	
Eternal vision and perspective	
Confidence and certainty	
Fullness	
God-sized purpose	
Praise	

Side by side, it is a stunning picture. In the moments in which we choose to settle for It'll Do Lane, the compromises and concessions we make don't seem to make a big difference. But each time we settle, we sacrifice a little more of the Immeasurably More God intends for us to embrace. The reality of It'll Do Lane is found in the broken dreams and shriveled souls that line its streets. It is a place of loneliness, weakness, restlessness, and instability. Blindness gives way to fear, worry, and anxiety. Emptiness drives the hearts that call It'll Do home to grasp for purpose and meaning in things that only make the soul hollow. There are no echoes of praise on It'll Do Lane.

God's Immeasurably More or It'll Do Lane? Jesus died on the cross so that you could live in the abundance of God's Immeasurably More. He paid the price so that you wouldn't ever have to settle. He is willing to work in your life today to help you move into the purpose God has always meant for your life. Settle or surrender – the choice is yours.

It'll Do Lane

It is just too good to be true. It is a nice picture in a Bible, but isn't something that can be a reality in my life. Hope hurts. It is easier to make my own place in the world, and deal with life as it comes. I may not have the greatest life, but it is my life and it'll do.

Immeasurably More

More than I can ask or imagine is an amazing reality to live in. God promises to fill my life with Himself and open possibilities that stretch into eternity. This is the life I was meant to live. It requires faith and surrender, but His heart is the only place I want my heart to call home.

Choosing a Home For Your Heart

Write Ephesians 3:20 and put it somewhere in which you can see it often. Use these words to ask God to help you imagine what His Immeasurably More might look like in your mirror. Ask Him to help you surrender to His dream for you.

Walk Called Lesson 9

Have you ever moved? Moving is a chore. Whether you are moving across the country or across the street, it requires you to pack up your stuff and relocate. You have to learn new rhythms, settle into new spaces, and develop new routines. It is a journey that makes a new home, both for your things and for your heart.

When you move, you have the opportunity to go through all of your things and reevaluate. Is this worth taking to the new place? Some things are obvious choices and get packed immediately. There are other things, though, that we throw out. They no longer fit, don't work properly, or are just out-of-date. In addition, there always seems to be a need to get some new things for our new space. New needs pop up. New habits require new equipment. It is exciting to turn a house into a home.

Having decided to embrace God's call into His Immeasurably More, it is now time to move. We will spend the rest of our time together packing, moving, and getting settled in our new home. We will learn how to best live in His Immeasurably More, and how to say good-bye to It'll Do Lane forever.

Day 1

The letter to the Ephesians naturally falls into two parts. Chapters 1-3 paint a beautiful picture and offer an amazing invitation into God's Immeasurably More. Each verse helps us catch a deeper glimpse into the abundant, rich life God dreams of pouring into our souls. Its words also help us see the life for which we so often settle. It reveals the heartbreaking reality of It'll Do Lane, even as it calls us into His Immeasurably More.

Immeasurably More

Chapters 4-6 help us change our focus and the address of our hearts. Having made the decision to live in God's Immeasurably More, Paul's words now help us move in. These three chapters contain practical, encouraging, and dynamic markers that guide us into the Immeasurably More life.

Write Ephesians 4:1.

Go back to the verse you just wrote out, and circle the word *walk*. Now define the word *walk*.

Walk is a movement word. By its very nature, it is the opposite of settling. This is why it is so important to the Immeasurably More life. *Walk* is going to be our key word for the journey into God's Immeasurably More.

Throughout the Bible, walking is one of the best descriptions for how God calls us to interact with Him. Adam and Eve walked with God in the Garden of Eden. Noah walked with God, finding favor in His eyes. Enoch walked with God, as did Job. The kings either walked with God or they walked in the ways of the world. One of the most profound pictures we have of a heart that walked with God is found in Abraham. While Adam and Eve show us what we lose when we settle for less than God's best, Abraham helps us see the incredible blessings of walking with God. Meshing his life with Ephesians 4-6 will define the markers that will help us move into His Immeasurably More.

Read Genesis 12:1-9.

What does God direct Abram to do?

How does God describe the Immeasurably More life He offers Abram?

How does Abram respond to God's invitation?

What does Abram do at the oak of Moreh, and again when he camps between Bethel and Ai? Why do you think he does this?

The Lord calls Abram to leave his home, his family, his country, and his life to follow Him into an unknown land. God offers Abram a future that is beyond what he can ask or imagine for himself. It requires that he surrender the life he can see in order to walk in a life defined entirely by the presence, provision, and protection of God. It is an extraordinary invitation. Leave everything and walk with Me. It is the same invitation He offers you and me.

There are four powerful walking lessons that we learn from this snapshot of God's call and Abram's obedience. They will help us get started on our journey into His Immeasurably More.

Listen to His Voice. We don't know how much knowledge or interaction Abram had with God before this moment in Genesis 12. We do know that when Abram hears the voice of God, he listened. He knew when God was speaking and turned his heart to respond to the voice that would define his direction and his devotion.

If we are going to live in God's Immeasurably More, we have to learn to listen to His voice. He is talking to you, calling you, beckoning you, entreating you, encouraging you, and speaking words of love to you right now. His voice echoes through the world, but only a few have tuned their ears to hear it.

How do we learn to listen more carefully for His voice?

Follow His Lead. Abram doesn't set out on his own. He follows the guidance of the Lord. He goes "to the land that I will show you." Too often, we start walking, but decide to set our own pace or walk in our own path.

Learning to follow His lead means learning to shadow His steps, surrender to His timing, and keep our eyes on Him.

What does the children's game 'Follow the Leader' teach us about following God's lead?

Take What You Need. When Abram started on his journey, he had to make some decisions. Genesis 12:5 says that he gathered the people he would take with him and packed up the possessions he would need for the journey. Abram walked prepared. He also walked away – away from his home, his family, places and routines that were a part of his life, and stuff that tied him to a life he was now called to leave. There were bags he packed, and baggage he left behind.

What might be something you need to leave behind in order to walk into God's Immeasurably More?

Build an Altar. Twice in two verses, we are told that Abram builds an altar to the Lord. Altars are places of worship, sacrifice, and dedication. Praise flows at altars. So might tears. It is a place where prayers ascend, hearts bend, and commitments are renewed. Those things are heart focuses that will be vital to walking in the Immeasurably More life.

Read Romans 12:1-2. How will spending time at the altar of worship and sacrifice help you walk as you have been called?

Day 2

God calls us to walk with Him. He invites us to join Him in His Immeasurably More and leave behind the emptiness of It'll Do Lane. In learning to listen to His voice and walk by His side, He calls us to bring the heart attitudes that will help us on the journey.

Read Ephesians 4:1-3.

What does it mean to walk in a manner worthy of your calling?

What attitudes does God want us to bring with us on our journey?

Walking with God is a privilege and an adventure. When we move in His steps and walk by His side, He will delight us and take us places we never would have imagined going on our own. The constancy of His presence is His greatest gift.

In order to best experience the fullness of His Immeasurably More, Paul encourages us to pack a set of attitudes and mindsets that will help us on the journey.

Packing is an interesting art. When we pack a suitcase, we reduce our lives down to a single bag. There are things that we name as necessary and they go in the bag. Other things get left behind because they won't aid us on the journey. These verses open up such a suitcase. They are the essentials. Here is what we most need to pack in our hearts if we are going to go the distance into God's Immeasurably More.

Perspective – The first thing Paul calls us to pack is perspective. We are to walk in a manner worthy of the calling to which we have been called. In order to walk in God's Immeasurably More, we need to have an understanding of the value of such a life. As we have already seen, walking in His way requires a constant stream of choices for the Immeasurably More life. The world will always give us reasons to settle. It'll Do Lane will call our names. If we are going to walk in a worthy way, we need to fix our eyes on our goal.

We need to change our priorities so that looking like Jesus is the greatest desire of our hearts. Everything else – every choice, every opportunity, every struggle, and every want – must be filtered through the lens of living in God's Immeasurably More.

How will asking, "Is this worthy of God's Immeasurably More?" help you measure the choices and opportunities that come your way?

Immeasurably More

Humility – Hearts that are humble are hearts that are willing to follow. Humility allows us to honor God as Lord. It opens the way for His leading, His timing, and His pace to take shape in our lives. Humility invites gratitude to lift our eyes and energize our steps. It gives wings to our praise and keeps our hearts closely tethered to His mercy.

What is the opposite of humility? How would carrying this opposite attitude have a detrimental impact on our ability to walk in God's Immeasurably More?

Gentleness – Closely tied to humility is gentleness. Gentleness is characterized by tenderness of heart. *Gentleness* is an interactive word. It showcases an attitude of responsiveness that is absolutely necessary if we are going to walk with God.

What is the opposite of gentleness? How would carrying this opposite attitude have a detrimental impact on our ability to walk in God's Immeasurably More?

Patience – Patience is essential for any journey. There is always a "how much longer?" element when we travel. The best definition of patience is found in the wisdom of waiting without whining. Learning to wait on God is imperative as we walk into His Immeasurably More. His timing must rule our steps. His wisdom must overshadow our hearts. Patience requires us to surrender our wills in order to live in the abundance of His will. It encourages us to be satisfied in His presence, rather than settling for being comfortable in our circumstances.

What is the opposite of patience? How would carrying this opposite attitude have a detrimental impact on our ability to walk in God's Immeasurably More?

Bearing with one another in love – Within God's Immeasurably More, we live as a connected people. We don't walk alone. We walk with God, but we also walk with the people called by His name. This is a beautiful blessing, but also demands a change in heart. My journey is not completely my own. What I do affects you. What you do has an impact on my walk with God. When we bear with one another in love, we pack a willingness to set self down in order to help someone else walk the walk.

What is the opposite of bearing with one another in love? How would carrying this opposite attitude have a detrimental impact on our ability to walk in God's Immeasurably More?

Eager for unity – Unity is one of the most definitive evidences to the world that Jesus stands in the middle of our lives. Left to our own devices, we gravitate in different directions, each defined by our own core of wants and desires. Peace unites us around a common purpose and gives us a common direction. It implants within us a desire to look beyond self, and celebrate the way the Spirit binds us together in the bonds of peace.

What is the opposite of being eager for unity? How would carrying this opposite attitude have a detrimental impact on our ability to walk in God's Immeasurably More?

It'll Do Lane

The urge to settle in and be comfortable in my own space is strong. I am doing pretty good where I am. Why walk into the unknown when I feel safe in the life I have created for myself?

Immeasurably More

God calls me to walk with Him. It is the journey of a lifetime. His call will change everything about my life. I will need to pack my heart with the things that will best help me experience the adventure He has in store for me.

Choosing a Home For Your Heart

Look at the packing list Paul outlines in Ephesians 4:1-3. Which of these heart attitudes do you need to pack more deeply into your life? Which opposite attitudes are slowing you down?

Day 3

The number one is a unique number. Within the number one, we have a picture of unity, wholeness, and singularity. It is the first whole number. The word *one* communicates the idea of a particular, of being undivided, and of distinctiveness. One is the next marker Paul introduces into our journey into God's Immeasurably More. God Himself is One and He calls us to one path, one purpose, and one plan.

Read Ephesians 4:4-6.

How many times does Paul use the word *one* in these verses? Why do you think there is such an emphasis on *one*?

Make a list of the "ones" God wants you to embrace.

One is not an entirely popular number in our society. One sounds restrictive. It speaks to limits, boundaries, and definition. Our culture places a high value on offering choices. The world promotes the idea that the more choices that are available, the more individual freedom can be exercised, and the more happiness will abound.

Working within this endless choice mindset, two different dangers arise. First, we can choose a path that leads us away from God's best. The choices the world offers encourage us to chase after our own desires, indulge our senses, and seek out the things that are the most satisfying in the moment. The second danger is more subtle. Sometimes, there are so many varieties, so many options, and so many possibilities that it paralyzes us. We don't know which direction to turn, which option will work best, or which way is the right way. The result is that we go nowhere. We settle for standing at the crossroads.

God answers the confusion that muddles our hearts with the wonderful word *one*. It is a word that provides clarity amidst all the distractions, compromises, and temptations that pull at our eyes. The clarity of His *one* helps us move in the right direction, aligns us with His purpose, and gives us a measuring stick with which to test the choices of the world.

How will having a clear focus on God's "ones" help you walk in His Immeasurably More?

These are the "ones" we can count on. There is one body, one Spirit, one hope, one Lord, one faith, one baptism, and one God and Father of all. All of these "ones" are united into One. Jesus is at the center of God's plan and purpose for your life. He is the One we are called to follow. Jesus is the Head of the body, His church. He is the One who gives us the Spirit to guide us as we listen to His voice. He is the source of our one hope. Jesus is Lord, the one Master that we heed. He calls us into one faith as we declare that He is the one and only Son of God. Baptism is the one path into His blood and the one way in which we are blessed with His grace. Jesus points us in one direction as He draws our eyes to the Father, empowering us to bring Him glory.

Keeping our eyes on God's "ones" will help us when are unsure of the next step. They work like signposts that help us follow His path and stay in His will. They set up the one direction we are to walk and point us to the one destination that makes the journey worthwhile – His heart.

When we are struggling with a decision point and are wondering which way to turn, the acronym **ONE** can help lift the fog created by all the world's choices and clarify the way into God's Immeasurably More.

Open His Word – The Bible is our very best source of information and guidance. In it, God opens His heart and invites us to be His children. He draws us a detailed picture of His character, reveals His nature, and lays out His purpose and plan for His people. The Bible is our roadmap, guidebook, and instruction manual. Every choice we make must be filtered through the wisdom and revelation of God's Word. If it aligns with God's Word, then we can be confident that we are walking in God's will.

Read II Timothy 3:16-17. How will staying engaged with God's Word help us walk in His Immeasurably More?

Notice Others – We walk connected. God places us in a family of believers so that we will have encouragement on the way, as well as examples that will help us stay on course. When we are struggling with which way to turn, godly people can help us find clarity. Their example becomes a source of light. Their wisdom points us to Jesus. United by a common hope and a common purpose, the faith of others can help us through the difficult moments that sometimes derail our journey.

Read Philippians 3:17. How will noticing the ways that others look like Jesus help us walk in His Immeasurably More?

Earnestly Pray – God wants you to walk with Him. It is His great desire for you to live in His Immeasurably More. When you are unsure or facing a difficult choice about which way to go, pray. Pray earnestly. Pray without ceasing. Pray for wisdom and direction. Pray for His Spirit to guide you. Pray for friends to walk alongside you. Pray for strength. Pray for the courage to wait on Him. Pray for the courage to take the next step He shows you.

Prayer positions our hearts for His answers. It opens our eyes to His presence. It gives us patience to wait for His movement and His power. In prayer, we surrender to His leadership and learn to wait on His timing. It lifts our perspective, and aligns it with the priorities of eternity.

Read Luke 18:1-8. How will earnestly praying help us walk in His Immeasurably More?

God's "ones" stand in contrast to the dizzying choices that the world throws at us every day. God very clearly marks the path into His Immeasurably More. There is one way to His one purpose and it goes through the One and Only Son.

Day 4

Christ calls us into His Immeasurably More. He tells us what to pack for the journey. He encourages us to keep our eyes on the One so that we will know the one way into His grace, the one source of our peace, and the one standard for our lives. As we start on our walk with Him, there is one more truth that He wants us to see as we take our first steps into His Immeasurably More.

Read Ephesians 4:7-16.

How was grace given to each one of us?

What picture of Jesus are we given in Ephesians 4:8-10?

For what four purposes does He give some to be apostles, prophets, evangelists, shepherds, and teachers?

1.

2.

3.

4.

Describe how we are to grow up into Christ.

Here is an amazing picture of the way Christ reaches deeply into our lives, making us His own. Grace is poured into our lives according to the measure of Christ's gift. It is His grace that touches our hard hearts, sin-encrusted souls, and misdirected motives and links our hearts to His heart. Grace cleanses us, revives us, and transforms us into a people called by His name and defined by His character. Yet, this grace is not generic or anonymous. It is personal, individual, and intimate.

God clearly sees the bruises left on your soul by the confines of It'll Do Lane. He knows your stubborn places, the weariness that tugs at your heart, and the scars of battles lost and hope abandoned. He gently applies the balm of His grace in exactly the way you need it in your life. He brings His transforming power to bear in your heart in precisely the way that is necessary to help you most look like Jesus. He moves in your life in an intimate, individual way because He wants to fill your soul with His Immeasurably More.

What does it mean to you to know that His grace is personally tailored to draw you into God's Immeasurably More?

Immeasurably More

Walking in the grace given to each one of us draws our eyes to our Savior. He is the one leader that we follow as we make the journey into His Immeasurably More. The world will offer us many voices that claim to know the way or have the answers. The television, radio, internet, and bookstores are filled with experts willing to sell you their advice for living an abundant life. Yet, the truth of God's Immeasurably More is wrapped up in Jesus. He doesn't want to sell you something. He longs for you to accept a gift. He doesn't need you to buy into an idea. He wants you to walk by His side. He doesn't want you to be a customer. His greatest desire is for you to be His child. So He gives us a victorious, triumphant leader to follow. Jesus has conquered sin, death, shame, guilt, apathy, and discouragement. He walked on this earth, witnessing first-hand the types of houses we build on It'll Do Lane. He descended into our piles of garbage, our mounds of excuses, our well-manicured justifications, and our comfortable complacencies. In order to fill us with all things, He emptied Himself of everything. Jesus stands as our leader into God's Immeasurably More. Any voice that does not lead us to Jesus is not a voice worth listening to.

As our Leader, He moves people into our lives who help us grow up into Him. They equip us for the journey. Through the body of Christ, He gives us the tools, knowledge, resources, and direction we need to walk in the manner He wants us to walk. The words of the apostles and prophets ring through His Word to draw us deeper into His holiness. Evangelists, shepherds, and teachers point us to Jesus, teaching us to recognize His presence, walk in His ways, and imitate His heart.

Name someone who has helped you look more like Jesus. Find an opportunity this week to thank them for helping you to know Jesus better.

The leadership God moves into our lives is designed to help us move in one direction. We are traveling toward one destination – to the measure of the stature of the fullness of Christ. Growing up in every way into Jesus is the goal of our journey. It is in Him that we will live most fully in God's Immeasurably More. Each step we take toward maturity is a step deeper into the abundance God purposes for us. The more intimately we know Jesus, the deeper our connection to the heart of God.

In walking as we are called, we walk connected. We are connected to Jesus by His grace. He is our Leader. In Him, we walk in the Way, are transformed by the Truth, and live in the Life He most desires for us.

We are connected to each other as the body of Christ. There is one body, and that body is uniquely designed to walk with Jesus. When we stay connected to that body, through prayer, worship, service, study, and fellowship, it is easier to avoid being tossed to and fro by the waves and winds of this world. Being connected to one another helps us stay anchored in Christ.

Examine your connection to the body. How well connected are you? What can you do this week to begin strengthening your connection to the body of Christ?

Love is the connective tissue that binds the body together. Love flows from the Head, because God is love. It is His nature and the pulse of His character. As His body, we take on His nature and invest ourselves in reflecting His heart. Love speaks the truth, pointing us to His very best. Love nurtures and cultivates, helping us grow up in every way. Love binds us together, connecting us to one another as traveling companions and fellow sojourners. Love equips us for living in the abundant life of God, encouraging us to invest our time, energy, creativity, and surrender in building the body up into the fullness of Jesus.

It'll Do Lane

I like the myriad of choices that I have in this world. I like picking my own path. It can be a little confusing sometimes, but I'll just keep listening to the 'experts' and figure it out as I go.

Immeasurably More

One is a word of comfort and peace. God is One and He calls me to one purpose, one path, and one plan. One opens up the abundance my heart desires. I will follow one Leader and walk toward God's one desire for me – looking like Jesus.

Choosing a Home For Your Heart

One is a whole number. Fractions are broken numbers. When we invest part of ourselves here and part of our hearts there, we end up broken, with pieces of our hearts invested in a little bit of this and a little bit of that. God calls us to devote ourselves to His One. Read Psalm 27:4. How can you cultivate this one desire in your life?

Walk Changed
Lesson 10

Remodeling always starts out sounding like a good idea. We looked around the room and knew that it was time. We made plans, picked out paint colors, and got excited about the possibilities to come. Then we started. We ripped up flooring, pulled down sheet rock, tore out cabinets, and demolished the fixtures. We looked around the room, wondering what we had done. Dust was everywhere, bare wall studs were the only visible structure, and gaping holes now stood as evidence of our remodeling enthusiasm. It looked terrible, and so far from the beautiful, bright, functional room that we had imagined.

Transformation of any kind has a moment like that. It begins with pulling out what doesn't fit, no longer works, is out-of-date, or needs to be replaced. Before the new can be installed, there is some demolition work that has to take place. Becoming like Jesus involves both tearing out what doesn't look like Him, as well as investing ourselves in taking on His nature and character. There will be days when we wonder if we will ever see the possibilities God sees in us, but in the end, something beautiful will emerge and take shape as we walk with Him.

Day 1

Moving from It'll Do Lane into God's Immeasurably More requires transformation. The move is a move of the heart. God's great purpose for you is to look like Jesus. Making that change in our lives requires some major remodeling. Sin has to be torn out, attitudes adjusted, motives made over, habits demolished and rebuilt, and function and purpose redesigned. It is the makeover of a lifetime. Today God looks around our hearts and assesses what needs to go in order to make room for the abundant treasure He wants to build into our lives.

Read Ephesians 4:17-19.

What change of direction do we require?

What about our minds need changing?

What about our hearts need changing?

What about our behavior needs changing?

Choosing to walk in God's Immeasurably More means choosing to walk in a different direction. That change in direction begins in repentance, turning us around and reorienting our hearts in the direction of God. Through obedience and surrender, we give up our place on It'll Do Lane and determine to live in the adventurous journey of walking with God.

Transformation is at the heart of God's vision for you. After living on It'll Do Lane for so long, we have accumulated a lifetime of habits, mindsets, attitudes, and motives that have to go. Changing a heart is more challenging than changing a room. But God has the expertise, the tools, the power, and the love to make His transformation a reality in you.

As we change direction and walk in our new life in Him, God notes key places in our minds, hearts, and behavior that need His transforming touch.

Our Minds

Our minds are our centers of understanding. The transformation that God wants to work in us requires a major shift in thinking. On It'll Do Lane, we saw the world through a specific lens. Our attitudes were shaped by our experiences. Our perception was formed by the landscape around us. As we learn to walk in His Immeasurably More, we have to surrender to a new mindset. We have to learn different ways of thinking, seeing, and measuring the world around us.

Four words jump out of these verses as God describes the elements of our minds that must be transformed. *Futility*, *darkened*, *alienated*, and *ignorant* are the "before" pictures God shows us as the remodel gets underway. Futility is the end result of living in darkness. Fruitfulness and hope can't blossom and grow in a mind that hides from the light of God. We are alienated from God because of ignorance. Connection is built on knowledge.

Write Romans 12:2.

Spending time in His Word is going to be the tool that God uses to transform our minds. His Word is light. It brings wisdom, understanding, hope, and vision to our souls. Every time we open His Word, we have an opportunity to be changed.

Our Hearts

Our hearts are places of responsiveness. They are the core of who we are, the part of ourselves that interacts with the world around us. Over time, It'll Do Lane hardens our hearts. It walks in our lives, leaving scars and requiring us to toughen up or live in deep pain. God snaps a picture of our callous, hard hearts and tells us that they need a radical remodel. Hearts that are calloused are not sensitive to the presence and power of God. Hard hearts lack the tenderness and vulnerability necessary to respond to His movement and great desire for us.

Peeling off callouses or breaking up hard places is never fun. Learning to be sensitive and tender is difficult after years of building up defenses and being in a mode of self-protection. Spending time in His presence is the surest path to tenderness.

Our hearts change, soften, and grow when we soak them in the deep waters of His grace.

Read Psalm 51:10-12. How is the condition of our hearts connected to our awareness of living in the presence of God?

Our Behavior

The result of a mind and heart that are out of sync with God is behavior that embraces sensuality. Sensuality focuses our minds and hearts on what feels good to us. It becomes our standard and our measuring stick for what is right. When our minds are grounded in darkness and ignorance, we follow the path to pleasure as our greatest good. When our hearts are calloused and hard to the presence of God around us, we walk down paths that feed our greed for impurity and lust.

We often think of sensuality in terms of sexual behavior, but sensuality is any gratification of the senses. It focuses our hearts and minds on pleasing the physical in the moment. God's transformation calls us to set aside the impurity we cling to and embrace a life of holiness.

Read I Thessalonians 4:1-7. How will immersing yourself in His holiness help you live in His Immeasurably More?

Day 2

Calling us into His Immeasurably More, God invites us to walk changed. It is a change that starts deep in the heart of who we are and expands outward as we take the steps into the abundant life He promises. Today, we stand with Abram as God calls him to be changed in a very personal, intimate way. It is a change that will mark Abram as God's friend and define for us what it means to walk changed.

Read Genesis 17:1-14, 22-27.

How old is Abram when God appears to him?

How is Abram to walk before God?

What kinds of promises will this covenant pour into Abram's life?

What is required of Abraham and his offspring as they walk in this covenant with God?

How quickly does Abraham obey the Lord?

Almost twenty-five years have passed since God called Abram to walk with Him. During that time, Abram has followed God into a new land, received amazing promises about his future, and made mistakes about trusting God's timing and power. Now, when Abram is ninety-nine years old, the Lord appears to him, calling Abram to walk deeper into God's plan and purpose for his life.

In God's invitation to Abram to walk before Him and be blameless, we see the essence of every invitation God extends to our hearts. God wants us to walk before Him. Walk in the revelation of who He is. Walk in His nature and in accordance with His character. Walk in the rhythm of His heartbeat. Walk in the awareness that God is always before us.

In walking before God, He empowers us to be blameless. This is the transformation that He longs to work in our lives. Enmeshed in the word *blameless* is God's vision for your life. We often see the call to be blameless or perfect and throw up our hands. There is no way that we can be wholly holy on our own. Sometimes our reaction is to dismiss God's call as impractical and unrealistic.

Read Matthew 5:48. In what way does Christ call you to the same standard that God called Abraham?

Yet it is in the call to walk before God that He shows us the path that will lead to being blameless. It is by His power that we have new hope. It is by His name that we walk as new creations. It is by His movement in our lives that we have the momentum to go forward into this new life. God gives Abraham Himself, and that is the key to the call of the covenant with God.

Calling him into this deeper walk, God tells Abraham that he must wear the mark of their covenant in his flesh. Abraham is to circumcise every male in his family as a sign of submission and surrender to the presence and blessings of God in their lives. Abraham quickly moves to obey, circumcising himself and all the males in his household that very day.

Circumcision is not just a physical act. It is a move of the heart. In removing the foreskin, they are to make their hearts tender and sensitive to the presence of God among them.

Read Deuteronomy 10:16. How is circumcision supposed to mirror a transformation of the heart?

Write Ezekiel 36:26.

Throughout Scripture, circumcision becomes a picture of removing what is hard, calloused, and unfeeling to make our hearts tender and sensitive to the words, commands, presence, and movement of God. God calls every person who is connected to Him to walk before Him and be blameless. Circumcision is a move of surrender and obedience. It opens our lives to His transformation and cements our hearts in His holiness.

Read Colossians 2:11-14. In what way are we called to circumcision today? How does this circumcision help us shed the hard, calloused hearts that keep us locked on It'll Do Lane?

In baptism, we are called to walk in the fullness of Christ. By His blood, we are made blameless and perfect before God. Baptism is a burial ground for the old, calloused, darkened heart that had given itself over to sensuality and sin. In the regenerative blood of Jesus, we are given new lives and new hearts. It is where the remodeling begins.

That power continues to work in our lives to shape and transform us as we walk with Him. Every day a little more of the callous that hides my heart from God is peeled away. Each day I walk before Him, a little more of His light penetrates my soul. The process of walking into God's Immeasurably More is found in the daily surrender of my heart to His presence.

How does Abraham's willingness to be circumcised at age ninety-nine encourage you to open your heart to the transformation God wants to work in your life?

It'll Do Lane

Change is hard. It hurts. I am satisfied with being comfortable.

Immeasurably More

Moving into His Immeasurably More demands vulnerability and sensitivity to His presence in my life. It requires surrendering to the remodeling work He wants to do in me. The first step is to tear out the old, hard places that hide my heart from His. It can be painful, but I am already breathing in more of His deep, fresh abundance.

Choosing a Home For Your Heart

Hearts don't become soft on their own. They must be soaked in surrender, immersed in His presence, and bathed in His grace. Do a tenderness test. Read Psalm 119:9-16. The psalmist lays out a list of actions taken by a heart that longs to remain tender in His sight. How consistently do you engage your heart in these actions?

Day 3

Walking with God into His Immeasurably More means walking changed. He is working a transformation in our lives that will tear out the old and fill our hearts with His new. He brings in the tools of His Word, grace, and Spirit to rip off the callouses that hide our hearts from Him, and begins the work of recreating the image of Jesus within us. Today He shows us the tape measure that He will use to complete the job.

Read Ephesians 4:20-24.

Immeasurably More

What do we find in Jesus?

What are we to put off?

What are we to put on?

In contrast to the manner in which we used to walk, God calls us to walk in accordance with the truth that is in Jesus. Formerly, we walked according to our own desires, following the path of sensuality and indulging ourselves in anything that came along that met our fancy. In God's Immeasurably More, we live by a different standard.

What is a standard?

A standard is a measuring tool. It is an authority or principle by which we test what is true. The standard becomes our model or pattern. It helps us determine what is excellent and right. If something doesn't measure up against the standard, it is suspect and untrustworthy. If we want to know if something is good and reliable, we hold up against the standard and judge its value.

Our standard is Jesus. The truth that is found in His life and words becomes the guiding principle by which we must measure everything in our lives.

Our words must be set against His words. Our actions must be measured by His actions. Our motives must be judged by the standard of His heart. Our choices must be lined up next to His choices to see if they are right and true.

Measuring is important in remodeling. You can't approximate and get it right. Your best guess won't do. You can't eyeball it and hope it comes out right. You have to get out a tape measure and a level in order to complete the task, and have everything fit and function like it is supposed to.

That physical picture gives us a profound insight into a deep spiritual truth. Our world will tell us that we don't need a standard. Do whatever feels right. Follow your heart. Go where the crowd goes. Each move based on our own approximation of what is right sets us up for failure. We end up disillusioned, disappointed, and with another layer of callouses on our hearts. The standard of truth that we find in Jesus never changes. It doesn't shift with what is popular or change measures according to the whims of society. It doesn't rely on my limited perspective, but grounds itself in eternity. It doesn't choose the easiest or most comfortable path, but the path that leads to goodness, holiness, and integrity.

Read John 8:31-32. How will the truth set us free to live in God's Immeasurably More?

It is against the standard of Jesus that we must line up our lives and take measure of our hearts. As we stand in Jesus, His truth acts like a mirror, helping us determine what must be taken off and put on in order to walk changed.

There are going to be things in our lives that when measured against the standard of Jesus have to go. Anything that is corrupt with deceitful desires is incompatible with the truth of Jesus. Corruption points us to the truth about our hearts. When something is corrupt, it is infected or tainted. It has moved away from the truth and been skewed by something else. That is where our deceitful desires lead us down the wrong path. Every day we face choices in which our desires make a prominent bid for us to follow. What we want in the moment can be so blinding that it is hard to see the pitfalls and compromises we are making. Because we are satisfying our own urges, it can be difficult to know that the choice is wrong until it is too late.

The standard of Jesus is our answer. When we keep our eyes fixed on Him, He becomes the measuring stick by which we test every choice and opportunity. Will this activity, behavior, choice, or conduct help me look more like Jesus? If the answer is no, we need to put it off and walk away. If the answer is yes, then it is something to enjoy and embrace.

Read Galatians 5:16-26. How do the lists of the works of the flesh and the fruit of the Spirit provide a standard with which to measure what is true in Christ?

Immeasurably More

Use the lists that you looked at in Galatians 5:16-26 to test a choice that you are struggling with today. How will measuring that by the standard of Jesus help you choose what is true?

Taking off the things that don't look like Jesus is only half of the transformation story. In addition to putting off what isn't true, God calls us to put on the new self. That new self is special. It is created after the likeness of God. It holds within it the image of Jesus. It pulses with righteousness and holiness. God doesn't just tear out the old, leaving it in shambles with big gaping holes. He calls us to walk changed. To replace the old with His new. To trade the deceitful for what is true. To walk in His will rather than our own desires.

Read II Corinthians 3:18. How is God transforming us for His glory?

Day 4

The call to walk changed is the call to be transformed. God's Immeasurably More takes shape in our lives when we allow Him to move in and begin remodeling our hearts. He has a vision for your life that is wrapped up in the image of Jesus. Using Jesus as our standard, He calls us to put off what is contrary to His nature, putting on what is consistent with His righteousness and holiness.

Read Ephesians 4:25-32. Use the passage to create a picture of what we are to put off and put on in Christ.

Put Off	Put On

Which of the characteristics in the "Put Off" list do you most urgently need to remove from your life?

Which of the characteristics in the "Put On" list would you like to build up in your life?

Now the remodeling plan gets down to specifics. Having laid out our standard, the Holy Spirit moves in to help us take a closer look at our hearts. Jesus is our pattern, and everything in our lives must be measured against His righteousness and holiness.

The first thing that must go is *falsehood*. Lies can be whoppers or subtle shadings. Lies of any kind are contrary to the One who is Truth. Lies break relationships and set themselves up on illusions. When we speak the truth, we honor the intimacy that comes from being connected in Christ. We are all members of one another, and the truth I speak to you impacts us all.

The way we handle *anger* becomes another place of surrender. In our world, anger gives us license for all kinds of resentment, bitterness, and revenge. Anger becomes an excuse and justification for bad behavior. In the Spirit, God calls us to surrender our anger to His sovereignty. Anger is an emotion. We will be angry. Anger is not a sin. It is in letting anger take up residence in our lives that gives the devil an open door to come in and have a foothold.

How does the instruction not to let the sun go down on our anger help us surrender our anger to God?

People who live in God's Immeasurably More are not *thieves*. They do not steal from others, whether physically, emotionally, or morally. Someone who steals declares with every move that God is not faithful enough, trustworthy enough, or resourceful enough to provide. This kind of thievery shows up when we determine that we must provide for ourselves any way we can. Instead, God calls us to not only honest work, but generosity also. We are people who are defined by integrity and openhandedness.

Immeasurably More

Living in God's Immeasurably More will be evident in the way we *talk*. No rotten, corrupting, or unwholesome words will come out of the mouths of those who have moved out of It'll Do Lane. God's children understand the power of words. They have the ability to build others up, strengthen weary souls, and provide stepping stones of grace and wings of hope for hurting hearts.

Read Matthew 12:34. What do your words reveal about your heart?

Walking changed means that we fundamentally change the way we interact with God. His delight is in the forefront of our minds. His desires shape the direction of our hearts. His joy fuels our steps. His grief stops us in our tracks, causing us to reexamine our focus and bow in repentance.

God's presence in our lives is the greatest blessing of the Immeasurably More life. Our awareness and sensitivity to that presence is one of the most crucial markers of a heart that looks like Jesus.

Who do you know that is especially tender to the presence of God in their lives? What do you learn from them about how to delight the Spirit?

Putting away bitterness, wrath, anger, clamor, slander, and malice is essential to the transformation of our hearts. Bitterness quickly takes root in our lives, choking off joy. Wrath and anger keep us in an uproar, always looking for the advantage rather than opportunities to serve and share. Clamoring carries with it the picture of someone who is always picking a fight or causing a disturbance, instead of being a peacemaker or inviting stillness. Slander seeks to tear someone else down to your own advantage. It doesn't leave room for grace or encouragement. Malice is just meanness. It speaks to evil intent and a desire to harm others out of spite. Love has no place in a heart filled with malice.

In their place, we are to make a deliberate move into Christlikeness. Kindness dictates our interactions with others. Compassion opens our eyes to the needs of those around us, while tenderheartedness allows us to be touched by the heart of others. As the forgiveness of Jesus pours into our lives, it creates a well of grace that can be poured out on those we meet. The life of Jesus becomes our standard and the measure by which we live every part of our lives.

It'll Do Lane

I set my own standard. I can decide what is right or wrong for me. No one else really has a right to tell me what to do. I am good person. My decisions don't really affect anybody but me.

Immeasurably More

Living in God's Immeasurably More means bringing everything into conformity with Jesus. I measure everything against His truth. Walking changed means putting away the things that don't look like Him and letting God build the likeness of Jesus in every part of my life.

Choosing a Home For Your Heart

If you want to measure an inch, you pull out a ruler. If you want to measure your life, you have to use the standard of Jesus. The "whatever" list in Philippians 4:8 provides us with a handy ruler by which to measure the choices and opportunities that come our way. Write Philippians 4:8 on a card and carry it with you. If what you are measuring can pass the Philippians 4:8 test, it looks like Jesus. Embrace it and enjoy it.

Walk Closely
Lesson 11

Do you have a best friend? Thinking about my best friend makes me smile. We have a neat relationship, and thankfulness overwhelms me as I think through the blessings that are mine because of my friend.

God uses our friends to give us pictures of what it means to walk with Him. Friendships require time, transparency, commitment, sacrifice, and trust. Friendships first start to grow because we share common ground. It may be a shared interest, experience, location, or circumstance. From there, deep friendships take root because of the investment each friend is willing to make in the relationship. We give each other time as we share our hearts. We commit to guarding the soul of the other as transparency allows us to truly see the other person. Sacrifice is one of the languages of friendship as each friend offers what is special to nurture the relationship.

The best friendships have God at their core. In Him, friends can share in His Immeasurably More and the joy that comes from being connected to each other through His love. As He draws us closer to His heart, He calls us to be His friends and walk closely by His side.

Day 1

Abraham is named God's friend in James 2:23. That is the context in which we must examine the next piece of what it means to walk in God's Immeasurably More. Friendship provides the framework for understanding what it means to walk closely with God.

Read John 15:15. How does Jesus describe you?

Read Ephesians 5:1-2.

What does it mean to be an imitator of God?

How does God call us to walk with Him?

Imitator is such an expressive word to describe how we are to follow God. An imitator is a copier. When we imitate Christ, we are mirroring Him in our lives. We open our hearts up as a reproduction of His heart in us. Being an imitator requires closely watching the One we are imitating, soaking in His presence, immersing ourselves in His character, and duplicating His actions and movements.

Imitating Christ is going to lead us to walk in love. Everything Christ did was defined and shaped by love – from healing blind men, to rebuking the Pharisees, to calming the storms in both the sea and in the hearts of His disciples. The greatest evidence of His love is seen in His sacrifice. When He stretched out His hands and offered Himself in our place, He demonstrated a greater love than the world had ever known.

Imitation, *love*, and *sacrifice* become the key words in learning to walk closely with God. They are words we first see echoed in Abraham.

Read Genesis 22:1-19.

What does God call Abraham to do?

How does Abraham respond to God's command?

What declaration of faith does Abraham make as he journeys to the mountain?

How does God provide for Abraham?

How does Abraham's obedience open the door for him to walk deeper into God's Immeasurably More?

In a moment that echoes of a sacrifice yet to come, God calls Abraham to sacrifice his beloved son, Isaac. Isaac is the child of promise, the evidence of God's almighty power in the lives of Abraham and Sarah. Now, years after the promise was fulfilled, God calls Abraham to take this precious gift and return it to Him in sacrifice.

The way Abraham responds speaks profoundly of the relationship he shares with God. Having walked in very deep friendship for a long time, Abraham packs his bags and heads to the mountain. On the way, his faith shines with a brilliance that comes from spending much time in the Light. Speaking to Isaac, Abraham tells him, *"God will provide for himself the lamb for a burnt offering, my son."*

Abraham binds his dear son to the altar. An altar is a place of sacrifice, worship, commitment, and trust. All of these are poured out from Abraham's heart as he lifts the knife to slay Isaac. He is willing to sacrifice what is dearest to his heart because his friendship with God is dearer still.

In a moment of great beauty, God provides a ram for the sacrifice in Isaac's place. It is a moment which imitates the reality still to take place centuries later at Golgotha.

What does Abraham teach you about sacrifice?

What does this moment on Moriah teach you about what it means to be an imitator of God?

Abraham's willingness to sacrifice Isaac is a picture of pure surrender. It peels away every layer behind which we might hide, and shows us what it means to give ourselves fully to God. Nothing hidden, nothing withheld, nothing but trust in the One who calls.

We often view the picture at Moriah as one of the lengths Abraham would go for God. In reality, it is a picture of how far God is willing to go for us. It shows us what He is willing to do for love, friendship, and to open the door for us into His Immeasurably More.

Day 2

Living in God's Immeasurably More means learning to walk closely to God. That is the best way for imitation to take root. We have to be close enough to the One we are imitating to pick up all the nuances of their nature. In order to walk closely with God, we are going to have to follow Christ's example. Walking in love, He gave Himself as a fragrant and holy sacrifice to God.

God calls us to walk closely with Him in sacrifice because sacrifice opens our hearts to His presence. It cuts our ties to this world and frees us from the things that tend to bind our souls. Sacrifice is closely tied to worship. Moving deeper into God's Immeasurably More means taking inventory and asking what we are willing to sacrifice in order to most closely imitate Jesus.

Read Ephesians 5:3-6.

What must not even be named among the saints?

What kind of language is out of place? What needs to fill our mouths instead?

What two types of people can we be sure have no inheritance in the kingdom of God?

Altars are places of sacrifice and worship. It is at the altar that we align our hearts and fix our focus. The problem is that our hearts are fickle. We like to divide our hearts into pieces, offering them in small portions on altars of our own convenience and desire.

Most of us don't think of ourselves as idolaters. We would never bow down before an image of gold or silver, or think of giving our heart to a statute made of wood or stone. But idolatry is rampant. It attacks the root of our relationship with God, destroying our friendship and poisoning our hearts.

How does Ephesians 5:5 define *idolatry*?

Any form of greed or covetousness is idolatry. It is any unhealthy desire to which we give our time, attention, affection, or focus. For many of us, we don't give money, things, comfort, relationships, food, shopping, recreation, media, or a hobby our full hearts. Just a piece. We let it control part of our lives, but in dividing our hearts, we have bowed to an idol and broken God's heart.

The Latin root of the word *covet* holds a picture that might help us better understand why greed grabs hold of our hearts. The Latin root of *covet* is *cupidiētāre.*[1] Do you see it? Cupid is at the heart of covet. It is an irrational love that pierces our hearts. Add the picture of *"the flaming darts of the evil one"* found in Ephesians 6:16, and it becomes even more clear how covetousness can disrupt our ability to walk closely with God.

It is within this context that God calls us to sacrifice. He challenges us to put anything on the altar that needs to be cut away from our lives. Many times the things that we need to sacrifice for the sake of our friendship with God are things that we enjoy, bring us pleasure, or even love.

Why is this kind of sacrifice necessary if we are going to live in God's Immeasurably More?

There are three categories of things that God calls us to bring to the altar of sacrifice – what we desire, what we love, and what we think.

Sexual immorality and impurity speak to the things that we *desire*. In chasing after impurity, we seek to satisfy our desires in ways that are outside of the will and purpose of God. The thrill of immorality – of whatever sort – becomes our motivation. We use impurity to satisfy our desire for control, comfort, or companionship.

God tells us to put our desires on the altar and sacrifice them to His desire. He wants to satisfy us with His love and delight us with His desire, but first we must cut the desires that pull our eyes away from Him out of our lives.

Covetousness defines the things we *love* in an unhealthy way. These things often have a very subtle hold on our hearts. They are dressed up in our rationalizations and decorated with our justifications. We need it. We could walk away if we wanted to, but we don't want to right now. It is our "guilty pleasure." It is where we turn for comfort or to feel in control. God tells us that if it pulls at our hearts, it needs to go on the altar.

Read Matthew 10:37-38. What is Jesus teaching us about sacrifice and the focus of our hearts in these verses?

Finally, filthiness, foolish talk, and crude joking reveal much about the way we *think* and where we have centered our minds. God wants us to offer our thoughts and our very words on the altar of His holiness. Our words speak volumes about how we see others, what we think about God, His presence, and His call on our lives. It is impossible to be crude and consecrated at the same time. Filthiness and faithfulness do not go together. When we talk foolishly, we reveal a mind that is disconnected from the wisdom of God.

Read II Corinthians 10:5. How do we take every thought captive for Christ?

In what way is thanksgiving one of the best sacrifices we can offer to God?

Gratitude pulls our hearts into alignment with the heart of God.

Thanksgiving opens our eyes to the movement of God and helps us be sensitive to the ways that He is touching our days. It directs our desires and fuels our contentment. It humbles our hearts, making God the source of our delight and the object of our love. Gratitude pushes unholiness away from our lips as our mouths seek to speak His praises. In thanksgiving, we see God. He fills our vision, thus He fills our hearts.

Write Hebrews 13:15.

It'll Do Lane

I want to be my own person. I don't want to imitate anybody. I know that there are things I should probably give up doing, but I am a good person. Why should I have to sacrifice the things I enjoy, that give me a little bit of comfort and feeling of control in this world?

Immeasurably More

God calls me to walk closely with Him in deep friendship. Friendships require sacrifice. I must be willing to set aside anything that gets in the way of the relationship. God sacrificed His Son so my sin wouldn't block our relationship. He gives me Himself. He calls me to sacrifice anything that pulls my heart away from Him.

Choosing a Home For Your Heart

Read Psalm 51:17. Spend some time praying about what God might be calling you to sacrifice in order to walk more closely with Him. Chances are you already know what it is. If so, ask Him to break its hold on your heart and to give you the courage to lay it on the altar and offer it to Him.

Day 3

Have you ever noticed how two people who walk together for a long time start to resemble each other? The closer two people walk together, the more they influence one another, share common hopes and dreams, and reflect each other's hearts. Again, we see a picture that points us straight to God. The longer we walk with Him, the more like Him we become.

Read Ephesians 5:7-14.

How has our identity changed in Christ?

What does it mean to walk as children of light?

How should light interact with darkness?

Some of the hardest things for us to sacrifice are the basic pieces of our identities. Our choices make up the foundation of our identity and how we interact with the world. We choose our jobs, our homes, our clothes, our haircuts, our cars, our spouses, our friends, and our educations. When we introduce ourselves to someone, we tend to tell them first about our choices and how those choices define who we are.

Walking closely with God is going to have a profound impact on our identities. The deeper we walk into His Immeasurably More, the more our identities are shaped and influenced by the character of Christ. As a result, there are going to be pieces of our identities that we will be called to lay on the altar and sacrifice in order to make room for the identity of Jesus to take shape in us.

When we become Christians, God makes a fundamental change in our identities. Once we were darkness, but now we are light and called to walk as children of Light. What once defined us is gone. Our old identities are consumed in the brilliant light of Jesus Christ. We are no longer defined by the world or our own choices. We take on the identity of the One who bought us with His own blood.

Read the following Scriptures. What identity does God give us as people who walk with Christ?

I John 3:1

I Peter 2:25

Romans 6:22

The common thread between all of these identities that we have in Christ is where the identities are formed. Children find their identities in family. They wear the Father's name, live in the Father's house, and live under the Father's authority. Sheep are led by a Shepherd. The Shepherd provides for and protects the flock. He decides when they lie down, what they eat, and where they go. Slaves live in the shadow of the Master. It is His will at work, His ownership that gives value, and His direction that we follow.

The same is true with light. Our identity as children of Light flows from the identity of Jesus as the Light of the World. We are light because He is Light. We are no longer shaped by the darkness. We don't make decisions about who we are based on what is pleasing to the world, what will make us popular, or how we can best get what we want. We try to discern what is pleasing to the Lord, aligning everything we are with what we see in Him.

Read John 8:12. What Immeasurably More promise does Jesus make to those who follow Him?

Our identity as children of Light not only tells us who we are and to whom we belong, it gives us a framework for how we are to interact with the world. In our society, there is a tremendous pressure to fit in. We value individuality as long as it conforms to the world's standards and doesn't go too far out of the box. We constantly measure ourselves against the people around us, making adjustments to our identity based on their reactions.

God wants us to remember that our standard is Jesus. Because Jesus is Light, we are children of Light. We no longer live on It'll Do Lane. God's Immeasurably More has given us a new address, a new perspective, and a new focus. It is not our purpose to blend into the darkness. Our identity is shaped by the choice God made to send His Son, rather than the choices that we make to chase our own desires. We no longer fit into the world in which we once lived. And we shouldn't try.

In what way does the world challenge you to compromise your identity in Christ?

Instead, our new identity comes with a new purpose. Light has the power to expose the unfruitfulness of darkness. It illuminates where others try to hide. It reveals the way home when darkness encourages walking down dead ends. Light heals and soothes where darkness causes fear and panic. Light promotes growth even as darkness turns hearts in on themselves. Light invites others to leave the darkness and take on the identity of Light Himself.

We don't always like to stand out. It is great in theory, but the reality is that most of us like to blend in with the crowd. It is more comfortable, less confrontational, and just plain easier. But light always stands out. You can see a small point of light in the middle of the darkness. Our eyes search for light. Our bodies crave light. Our souls were made for light.

As you finish today's lesson, sing the children's song "This Little Light of Mine" out loud. Think about your identity as a child of Light. Let the song encourage you to walk as light, live as a bright light in the darkness, and thrive as light in His presence.

Day 4

Learning to walk as children of Light means learning to walk in the identity that we have in Christ. Walking closely with God pulls our hearts ever deeper into His Immeasurably More. In Him, we find the joy, peace, purpose, and fulfillment that our souls crave. Living in His abundance requires a transformation of our hearts. His Spirit moves into our lives, remodeling and reshaping us into the image of Jesus. Our next move is to learn to make the consistent choice to walk closely with God.

Read Ephesians 5:15-21.

How are we called to walk?

How should we view time?

With what should we be filled?

How should we address one another?

Describe the way we are to give thanks.

How does reverence for Christ empower us to submit to one another?

Walking closely with God is a daily choice. Every day we get to choose how deeply we want to live in His Immeasurably More. Some days, it is easy. His presence is evident, His blessings are apparent, and our hearts open like a flower facing the sun. Other days find us struggling to keep in step with Him. We get distracted, discouraged, and drawn by desires that pull our hearts in a different direction.

Every day we have to choose how we are going to walk, where we are going to walk, and with whom we are going to walk. Living in God's Immeasurably More means learning to let His wisdom guide our steps.

Define *wisdom*.

God directs us to look carefully at how we walk. He wants our feet to be guided by His wisdom and shaped by an ability to choose His path with every step. Wisdom is the ability to consistently choose the right path. Wisdom is more than book learning, although knowing God and His will are essential to being wise. Wisdom also involves putting that knowledge into action and consistently making a choice for God.

Immeasurably More

The idea of consistency is imperative when we are seeking to move in wisdom. Making one wise decision is great, but walking wisely means consistently, steadily, regularly choosing His path. We can't enjoy the full abundance of His Immeasurably More until we consistently choose to live in His presence and in His way. The full benefits of wisdom are best seen in a life that practices wisdom consistently over time.

We understand this in the physical world. It is great to take a walk, eat a healthy meal, or practice the piano once. Those are good things, but the full benefit of those choices won't come into play with one healthy meal or practice session. It takes making a consistent choice to walk, eat well, or practice for the blessings of those disciplines to be evident in our lives. We are not healthy or considered musicians until those things are consistently a part of who we are.

What physical discipline or habit is a regular part of your life? What can you learn about walking in wisdom from the consistency of that discipline or habit?

Walking in wisdom means that we will consistently choose to walk in our identity as children of Light. His wisdom is going to evidence itself in our lives in several ways as we consistently choose to plant our hearts in His Immeasurably More.

Using Time – Walking wisely means that we will understand the value and gift of time. God created time to help us order our days, to understand His presence in our lives, and to help us see His movement. Foolish people squander time, missing opportunities to live fully in God. Wisdom makes the most of every day. This does not mean that we fill every moment with busyness. It means that we will live purposefully with a deliberate awareness that God is near.

Read Psalm 90:12. How do we learn to number our days?

Knowing God – Understanding the will of the Lord is imperative to walking wisely. We can't choose Him if we don't know Him. We can't walk in His way if we don't know where He stands. The only way to know someone is to spend time with them. Read His Word. Invest in prayer. Walk with His people. Be still in His presence.

Influence – Every day we make decisions about who is going to influence us. Are we going to let the world with its bent toward self-indulgence set the direction of our steps or are we going to open our hearts to the Spirit of God? The world is filled with experts who want to influence our choices, direction, purpose, and passions. Another option is to let things influence and shape us. It can be alcohol, drugs, food, sex, or money. The wise choice is to be filled with the Spirit of God. Let Him influence our actions, help us make our choices, and guide our steps.

What are you going to have to pour out in order to make room to be filled with the Spirit?

Conversation – Walking in His wisdom is going to be seen in the way that we speak to one another. A life grounded in His Immeasurably More is going to consistently choose to speak from a heart guided by God's wisdom and presence.

Our conversation is going to be filled with words that help us pay attention to His presence, bow to His sovereignty, surrender to the songs He wants to sing into our lives, and walk according to the rhythm of His heart.

How can singing help you consistently choose to walk in His Immeasurably More?

Gratitude – God keeps bringing us back to gratitude. It is a core characteristic of the Immeasurably More life. Thanksgiving shapes our perspective, aligns our focus, helps us enjoy the full measure of His abundance, and eases the tensions that tend to overrun our days.

Write I Thessalonians 5:18. How will you do this today?

Submission – Walking in God's wisdom is going to show itself in the way we interact with others. Submission calls us to lift Jesus up in reverence. In doing that, it changes our perspective of self and others. Walking wisely in submission means that we will consistently make the choice to point others to Jesus, even if that means meeting their needs before our own.

It'll Do Lane

I am who I am because this is who I choose to be. I like to make my own decisions and walk in my own wisdom. I would like to walk more closely with God, but don't really want to have to change everything about my life to do it.

Immeasurably More

I walk closely with God as a child of light. Each step draws me deeper into His presence and shapes me more into His image. In order to walk closely with God, I need to learn to walk in His wisdom. Every day I get to choose to experience more of His Immeasurably More.

Choosing a Home For Your Heart

Wisdom is the ability to consistently choose God's way. Do a consistency check. Do you consistently apply God's wisdom to the way you use your time? The people you let influence you? Your conversation? How deliberate are you about living in gratitude? In submission and reverence?

[1] "covet."

Walk Committed
Lesson 12

God made us to be a connected people. He designed us to live in community and find joy in the presence of other people in our lives. He also knows how profoundly those connections shape us. The people with whom we share our lives have intimate access to our hearts. It is within those relationships that our ability to live in His Immeasurably More will be most empowered or defeated. If we are going to live in the full richness of His abundance, we must commit to living in those relationships within the boundaries of His will.

Day 1

Marriage is precious. Within marriage, we live at our most transparent and our most vulnerable. Perhaps no other person has the power to help us live in God's Immeasurably More better than our spouse. And it is to the power of that relationship that God now speaks.

Read Ephesians 5:22-33.

With what attitude should wives interact with their husbands?

Immeasurably More

What parallel relationship does God point us to in order to help us understand a wife's connection to her husband?

With what attitude should husbands interact with their wives?

How do Christ's actions model the way a husband should treat his wife?

There is perhaps no subject that carries with it more baggage than a discussion of submission. It seems to either invoke guilt, nervousness, or outrage. All three are unnecessary. This section of Scripture is just like any other section of Scripture. It is inspired by God, which means that it contains truth that we need to live godly and righteous lives. It is written from the depths of His heart, meaning that it is framed in His love and is full of His goodness and grace. It holds His deep wisdom, meaning that it points us towards His best purpose for us which is the creation of the image of Jesus in our lives.

Define *submission*.

In order to lay down some of the baggage, let's first talk about what submission is *not*. Submission is not about being a doormat or giving someone permission to treat you badly. It does not mean that you don't have thoughts, opinions, or value. Submission is not a passive pose, or a license for avoiding responsibility. Submission is not the idea of an anti-feminist man written to a culture that holds no relevance for our own time. Submission is God's idea, God's best plan for your marriage, and God's tool for shaping you to more completely look like Jesus.

Submission simply means to yield. If you drive a car, you know what it means to yield. When two lanes become one, one car has to slow down and let the other car go first. That's submission. If one car doesn't yield, there is a collision. Damage, pain, injury, fear, and destruction result. Neither car gets to where it needs to go. Neither car leaves the moment in its best shape. When one car yields, both reach their destination.

Submission means that we live under God's control in our marriages. It is a position of the heart, a perspective of the mind, and an act of praise for the soul.

A Position of the Heart. Submission begins with bowing in surrender to God. Submission to our husbands is never separate from our surrender to the Lord. The way we interact with our spouses is a reflection of the way we interact with God. Surrendering to His authority gives Him access to our wills and our need for control. In releasing these into His sovereignty, it frees us to yield to our husbands.

Submission is the action of a heart that walks in the gracious freedom of His Immeasurably More.

We have no need to grab at control, hold onto the reins, or dictate our own path. Submission is an act of trust that declares that God is wise, good, and in control.

Read Philippians 2:3-8. What do the actions of Jesus teach you about living a life that is yielded to God and others?

A Perspective of the Mind. The world looks at submission and shakes its head. It is a perspective that can only be understood within the boundaries of God's great love. When we see submission only in terms of what we give up, we fail to see the beauty in God's plan for us. Submission is primarily about giving God access to our hearts and our most intimate moments. Marriage reveals our truest selves. It is where we are most open and unguarded. That is the person God wants to shape into the likeness of Jesus. When we refuse to submit, we are refusing to yield to God's deepest purpose for our lives.

Read Colossians 3:1-3. How will hiding our lives in Christ free us to live in submission?

An Act of Praise. We grumble and gripe about submission. In truth, it should be a source of deep gratitude. Submission is the movement of a heart that honors God. It is an act of praise lifted to the One who created us and calls us into His grace. Yielding in our relationships with our husbands declares that God is moving in our lives. In submission, we are given the privilege of looking like Jesus for the man to whom we have committed our lives and our love.

Husbands are called by God to love their wives as Christ loves the church. There is a tenderness and gentleness inherent in that call that we as women crave. God moves husbands into the position of protectors, leaders, and defenders. Sacrificial love is to define every movement, action, attitude, and motive. God's grace overwhelms his life as deep delight flows from nurturing and cherishing his wife as his own body. As the two become one, both partners are given the responsibility to guard the relationship and make it a place where the mystery of Christ is revealed to the world.

But here is one of our hang ups about submission. We look at our husbands and think that it would be easy to be submissive if they acted like they were supposed to act. If he treated me with that kind of love and consideration, I could respond in submission and all would be well.

In God's ideal, both marriage partners interact with each other in the fullness of God's grace and purpose. Husbands love their wives more than themselves, lead with the humility and sacrificial mercy of Christ, and cherish their wives as a gift from God. Wives joyfully submit and thrive under the tender care of a husband who loves her as Christ loves the church. That is God's plan. He wants both husbands and wives to look like Jesus with each other and to the world.

But submission is not the end result of God's plan. It is the process that takes us there. In order to move forward, someone has to yield. Our submission is not dependent on our husbands' actions. The directive to live in submission is not negated because our husbands' actions don't mirror the actions of Christ. Submission means that we live under God's control in our marriages, whether our husbands are living there or not. Our willingness to yield is entirely dependent on our surrender to God.

Read II Corinthians 9:6-11. What lessons does this passage hold for generously giving our submission to our husbands?

Day 2

God calls us to walk committed – committed to Him, committed to our husbands, committed to our children, and committed to living out His character with everyone with whom we come into contact. When we walk committed, we are opening our lives up for our commitment to God to overflow into every relationship we have.

Read I Peter 3:1-6.

How are wives called to live with their husbands?

What power do your actions and choices hold?

Describe the beauty that grows in a heart that is fully surrendered to God.

In what way does God use Sarah's life as an example for us?

In this passage, God connects our submission to beauty. It is a neat picture. Women long to be beautiful. Our definition of beauty may vary by culture, but our desire for beauty is God-born. Our world has taken that desire and made it entirely about physical appearance. Too many times, we buy into that definition and judge ourselves by the covers of magazines or the celebrities we see on television. Here God realigns our focus, teaches us how to walk committed, and draws us into His Immeasurably More.

Beauty begins with being dependent on God. Beauty that is dependent on God is beauty that gives up self-reliance, self-determination, and self-focus. It plants itself in the heart of God, sending its roots down deeply into His love and grace.

Submission boldly proclaims that God is in control. It calls us to bend our hearts to Him, allowing Him to shape the circumstances, people, and situations around us. It is in the context of our most private actions that the truth of our surrender shines most brightly. The purpose of our submission is to allow God to shape the image of Jesus deep within us. As He takes hold of our lives, others will be able to see Him in our actions, behavior, choices, and attitudes. The first one to notice should be our husbands. We don't have to nag, call attention to ourselves, or whine. Submission allows God to speak without our words getting in the way.

Immeasurably More

How do purity and respectful reverence help us live yielded lives?

Beauty is seen in a woman who is deliberate about her connection to God. These verses about beauty challenge us not to settle for the definition of beauty sold by the world. It doesn't mean that we can't wear make-up, jewelry, cute clothes, or uncomfortable shoes. It does mean that God has a bigger, deeper, Immeasurably More beauty in mind for you. He doesn't want you to settle for living on the surface when the beauty He has designed for you goes soul-deep.

A woman who walks committed to God uses her physical beauty to frame the beauty of Christ. She understands that beauty begins with her dependence on God in the inner person of the heart and radiates outward. Start in the right place and you will possess a beauty that will take the world's breath away.

God's definition of unfading beauty centers on a gentle and quiet spirit. It is a picture of a spirit yielded first to God. This kind of beauty is of great worth in His sight.

What does it mean to have a gentle and quiet spirit?

Possessing a gentle and quiet spirit is at the heart of submission. A gentle spirit leans completely on God. Humility, kindness, and surrender define gentleness. Its opposites are pushy, hard, demanding, and self-focused. A gentle heart has learned that God will supply every need. There is no reason for her to demand her rights or grab at control. God's sufficient grace becomes her greatest resource.

A quiet spirit has learned to rest in the presence and purpose of God. There is no need for the spotlight, no clamoring for attention, and no demand that it all be about me. A quiet spirit blunts the whining, worry, and moodiness in which we too often indulge. It knows how to be still before God and is committed to listening to Him.

How will committing ourselves to having a gentle and quiet spirit impact our ability to submit?

Beauty is seen in the lives of women dedicated to living in the presence of God. We don't know very much about Abraham's wife, Sarah. We are given only incomplete glimpses of her in the record that tells us of Abraham's walk with God. Yet, this passage tells us a great deal about the woman who shared a life with God's friend.

Sarah was a holy woman. Holy women dedicate themselves to living in the beauty of God's character. Holiness is at the heart of who God is, and He calls us to make holiness the foundation of our hearts as well.

Sarah was a woman of hope. Hope allows us to look for God's fingerprints on every moment, no matter what the moment holds. Hope lifts our eyes and helps us understand that life is deeper and goes far beyond what we can see in the moment.

Sarah understood the connection between beauty and submission. Sarah is called a woman of great beauty in Genesis 12:11. Yet, Sarah's greatest beauty is seen in the way she made herself beautiful as she adorned herself in submission.

In what way is submission a part of your beauty routine?

Peter tells us that we are Sarah's daughters if we do what is good and do not give way to fear. Submission calls us to consistently do the right thing as we walk in God's wisdom and purpose. We don't just submit when it is easy, comfortable, or convenient. We do what is right because it calls us deeper into the presence and purpose of God.

Fear stalls us and paralyzes our ability to walk committed. Too many times we fear that submission means being taken advantage of, taken for granted, or losing ourselves. Instead, Sarah's daughters choose courage, confidence, and joy. Deliberate in our dependence on God, we find our delight first in Him, and then in our relationships with others.

It'll Do Lane

Submission calls me to give up too much of myself. If I don't take care of myself, no one else will. I have to guard my heart, protect my rights, and demand my way.

Immeasurably More

God calls me into His Immeasurably More through the path of submission. He wants my marriage to be rich with His presence and a deep well of grace and transformation. He calls me to yield, first to Him and then to my husband, as I learn to walk committed to His love.

Choosing a Home For Your Heart

Struggling with submission is a normal part of the transformation process. It isn't easy to surrender your will or yield to another. Every woman holds a different kind of beauty, so your submission will not look exactly like someone else's, although it will always look like Jesus. The beauty of submission is developed in small, daily moves. What are three small actions you can take today to open your heart to deeper submission?

Day 3

Having spoken to the hearts of our marriages, God now calls us to walk with Him into the relationships with our children. Children are a priceless gift from the Lord. Blessings, beauty, and bountiful joy flow from watching our children grow. Parents carry a great responsibility into their connection with their children. Each moment with our children gives us the opportunity to point them to God and instill God's deep purpose in their lives.

Read Ephesians 6:1-4.

In what two ways does God call children to walk in submission?

What does it mean to honor your father and mother?

What warning does Paul give to fathers? What do you think this means?

What instruction is laid on the hearts of parents?

God's discussion about surrender and submission continues on as He turns our eyes to the relationship between parent and child. We are all children, even if we are not all parents. There is something amazing about the connection between parents and children. It transcends circumstances, struggles, heartache, joy, and the passage of time. Within the boundaries of this unique relationship, God calls us to seek His wisdom, live in His purpose, and experience His Immeasurably More.

Children are called by God to obey their parents. Obedience is a training tool of the heart. It teaches us to listen, trust, and act in the wisdom of another. Parents are to use obedience as a way to introduce their children to the sovereignty of God. As the first authority figure in a child's life, a parent helps a child learn what it means to respond to authority and set their will aside to follow a greater plan.

How can learning to obey a parent you can see teach you to obey your Father you cannot see?

The second call to submission directs children to honor their parents. Honor encourages us to treat our parents with respect, integrity, and consideration. In honoring our parents, we acknowledge God's hand on our lives. We learn how to honor God by honoring the parents with which He blessed us.

Immeasurably More

Not all parents are great parents. There are some parents who are easy to honor. Their actions point us to God and fill our lives with markers which make Him simple to follow. Other parents make it difficult to see God. Their behavior is warped by self-centeredness and displaced focus. Again, the call to honor is a call to submission. Our obedience to this command is not dependent on our parent's actions nearly as much as it is on our relationship with God. In honoring our parents, we are called to do what is absolutely best for them, while pointing them to Jesus.

Honoring our parents takes on different forms as we mature and our parents age. What piece of advice would you give someone younger than yourself about how to honor their parents at your age?

Parents are called to submission in their relationships with their children as well. We are to submit to God's authority as we raise our children to follow Jesus. We are not to misuse the authority God gives us in our children's lives. Parents have a tremendous opportunity to shape a child's view of God's heart and character.

Unstoppable love, consistent discipline, unquenchable delight, selfless sacrifice, unending prayer, and an open Bible are the best gifts that a parent can give to their children. Everything we do should focus on helping them look like Jesus.

Read Genesis 18:19. Why does God choose Abraham?

Read Deuteronomy 6:4-9. What do these words teach us about bringing up our children in the discipline and instruction of the Lord?

Teaching our children begins with our own hearts. We must love the Lord with all of our hearts, souls, and might. His presence must penetrate every part of who we are. His power must be at work in our hearts, shaping and transforming us into the likeness of Jesus. His Word must be our standard, and His grace our greatest joy. We have to be living lives of total devotion in front of our children. We can't let compromise infect our commitment. We can't point our kids to God's Immeasurably More if we are living on It'll Do Lane.

As we surrender to the way God wants to work in our lives and the lives of our children, we will write His words on our hearts. They will become a part of who we are. They will author the narrative of our lives, shaping the direction of our stories. His words will be living and evident in our hearts. Our children will be able to see the Word of God lived out in the reality of our lives. When we talk about forgiveness, repentance, and confession, they will have a three-dimensional picture alive in front of their eyes.

What is one way in which you can show someone that the Word of God is alive in your heart this week?

Once we are firmly engaged in walking committed with God, we invite our children into the process. We are to teach our children diligently. Diligence focuses us on being deliberate and purposeful. This is where our consistency is most evident and most closely watched. Training our children is an all-encompassing task. Every moment provides opportunities to show them God, point out His power, reveal His care, and help them take steps of faith. We talk about God when we sit down. We trace His fingerprints when we walk along the road. We engage them in prayer at bedtime, and help them walk in gratitude and surrender each morning when they wake up.

The Immeasurably More life opens up for our children when they see the life of Jesus in our hands as we serve. Children pay attention to our eyes, watching what we choose to watch and observing how we let the standard of Jesus measure what we see. The doorframes of our houses become doors into life with Christ where our children witness how we live out faith in the everyday. Our gates testify to the way in which we let Jesus direct our steps and determine where we go.

Children are commanded to be submissive to parents who are fully surrendered to God. In this way each generation learns the beauty of faith, the power of grace, the depth of love, and the wonder of living in His Immeasurably More.

Read Psalm 78:4-7. How will you share the Lord with the next generation?

Day 4

Living in God's Immeasurably More reaches out from our lives to touch the lives of others. It impacts our marriages and our children. It will touch our friends and neighbors. It will affect the person we meet at the grocery store and the person we hug at church. When we walk in God's Immeasurably More, it overflows into the people with whom we connect and interact.

Read Ephesians 6:5-9.

How are we to interact with our earthly masters?

How is our submission to earthly authorities meant to turn both our eyes and their eyes to the Lord?

In what way are those in authority to interact with those who serve under them?

The call to submission extends beyond our immediate family to the other circles in which we walk. Our surrender to God is supposed to be evidenced in any relationship in which we have to respond to the authority of another. We all live under authority. We live in a land with laws and government; authorities who help us live in peace with others. We go to schools, shop in stores, and volunteer in places that have rules and guidelines. Each of these hold some authority over our lives. The most common ground on which we walk under authority outside of our homes is in our work places. In each of these situations, we are called to let our submission to authority point others to the higher authority under whom we live our lives.

When we enter a situation in which we are under authority, we are to bring the perspective of Christ into the moment. We are to treat our earthly master – our boss, the police officer, the government official, or the volunteer organizer – with respect and fear. We are to have a proper view of authority, its value, and the responsibility that lies on the shoulders of the one in charge. Our respect will be evident in the way that we both interact with the person in charge and our exchanges with people who walk with us under authority.

We are supposed to bring our service into the moment with a sincere heart, as if it is Christ Himself that we are serving. Our surrender to God allows us to see Him in our workplaces, on the roads, in the stores, and where we give our time.

What we offer in service to others is, in reality, surrender to the One who claims us as His own.

Read Genesis 39:3, 21-23. What could others see by the way Joseph did his work?

In what way can others see that the Lord is with you in the way that you do your job?

The next piece of our surrender to those to whom we are under authority speaks to our integrity. We are not to be people-pleasers or to only be submissive when someone's eye is on us. God's people are to be people of integrity. We pour out the same effort, extend the same grace, and function with the same honesty and intensity whether someone is watching us or not.

Read Daniel 6:4-5. How does Daniel's integrity point others to his relationship with God?

Why is integrity an essential characteristic of those who live in God's Immeasurably More?

Immeasurably More

Of course, the call to walk in surrender is not just given to those who live or work under authority. Christians who find themselves in a position of authority hold a tremendous responsibility and privilege. We are to use that authority with humility and the realization that we, too, have a Master. If God came and washed feet, we can do no less than to treat others with dignity and respect.

The Immeasurably More life frees us from the games of power and control that dominate so much of our world. When we choose to live under the authority of God, every other authority in our lives becomes an avenue by which we honor the One to whom we have surrendered everything.

It'll Do Lane

It is a climb or be climbed on world. You have to be willing to push your way in or you will get pushed around and pushed out. Everyone else is just out for themselves. If I don't take care of me, who will?

Immeasurably More

God calls me to live out my surrender in every arena of my life. My children need to see my surrender so that they can learn what it means to walk committed with God. Living in His Immeasurably More demands that I be a person of integrity and submission wherever I am.

Choosing a Home For Your Heart

Those with whom we work and walk should be able to see our faith in our actions, choices, and attitudes. Read James 2:18-24. How does this passage connect faith with the surrendered way you walk in the world? Can someone see your faith by the way you work?

Walk Confidently
Lesson 13

God wants to give you more than you can ask for or imagine. He has an Immeasurably More life waiting just for you. It is a life of abundance, joy, peace, and grace. It is a life saturated with His presence, immersed in His purpose, and overflowing with His power. It is meant for you. He died so that you can have access to it. He lives to invite you to walk by His side. You just have to decide that you want to live it.

The world will tell you that you don't need it. It will whisper that you aren't good enough, smart enough, pretty enough, or deserving enough. It will advertise that it has a better deal - a house on It'll Do Lane. It can be all yours. All you have to do is settle.

The journey into God's Immeasurably More requires one more thing. We have to walk confidently. Confident in who God is, who He tells us we can be, and in His ability to transform us from the inside out. Confident that He gives us the ability to turn away from the sales pitches of the world, our own selfishness, and the settling mindset. Confident that the life He has planned for us is Immeasurably More than we can ask for or imagine.

Day 1

Here is the bottom line. The world does not want you living in God's Immeasurably More. When you make the decision to move out of It'll Do Lane and into God's abundance, the world sets its sights on bringing you back to where it is most comfortable. The forces of the world have a pretty big stake in keeping you right where you are. As long as everyone thinks that It'll Do will work, the hunger for more is just a quiet ache in the middle of the night. When someone actually lives the Immeasurably More life in front of others, it opens up the possibility that it might be meant for them as well. The potential of a mass exodus out of It'll Do Lane becomes a real threat. So a campaign begins, and you are the target.

Immeasurably More

Read Ephesians 6:10-12.

Write Ephesians 6:10.

What does God give us to put on?

How will God's provision protect us?

Describe the enemy.

God has a purpose and a plan for you. He wants you to live a bigger, richer, more abundant, more joyful, more alive life than you can ever imagine for yourself. He opens the door into His Immeasurably More through the body of His Son and invites you in. It is all yours. It requires obedience, sacrifice, and the willingness to live in the boundaries of His grace, but God uses even your surrender to push back the limitations of what is possible, empowering the impossible to take shape in your life. It is an amazing gift, and a wonderful life.

Satan has a plan for you too. Here in Ephesians, it is called a scheme. A scheme is a devious, underhanded plot. It is a conspiracy formed around intrigue with the purpose of luring someone away from the truth or tricking them into an action they might not have taken on their own. A scheme is the work of someone who is selfish – someone who is watching out for their own interests.

Read Genesis 3:1. How is the serpent described? What does this word mean?

Over and over again, the moment in the Garden of Eden is played out. We stand in God's Immeasurably More, enjoying the full blessings of dwelling in His presence. In creeps the serpent. Cunning and crafty, he has one objective. Convince you that you would be better off on your own than residing in the house of God's love. He packages It'll Do Lane with ribbons and bows, advertising it as a paradise of personal choice and absolute independence. And the battle begins.

God tells us that the only way to face these moments is to stand in His strength. On our own, we are just as vulnerable as Adam and Eve in the garden. Our fruit tree might look like a credit card, refrigerator, internet connection, television program, bottle, candlelight, or mirror, but he will find it. We don't have the strength to fight the way his lies worm their way into our hearts. Our only hope is to stand in the strength of God.

You see the battle really is bigger than you can imagine. For all of the reality of our physical world, it is just a shadow of the spiritual realm that surrounds us. We tend to think of ourselves as insignificant and not worth much notice. But the truth is that rulers, authorities, cosmic powers of darkness, and the spiritual forces of evil have their sights on you. Why? Because when you stand with God, you offer others the one thing the devil can't fight – hope.

The good news is that God is bigger and stronger than the devil. Within the promise of His Immeasurably More, He has already pledged that His power will work in you and through you for His glory.

Read Ephesians 1:19-23.

Describe the immensity of God's power.

Describe the breadth of Christ's triumph.

Who stands at the focal point of God's immeasurable power?

Day 2

God doesn't want you to face the devil's schemes with fear and anxiety. He is ready and willing to clothe you with His peace and His power. He wants you to walk confidently in His grace, knowing that there is nothing you will face today that He has not already seen and provided for.

Read Ephesians 6:13-17.

What does God provide for us that will help us stand firm in the evil day?

What is the nature of the different pieces of armor God gives you?

Belt of ______________________________

Breastplate of ______________________________

Shoes which put on ______________________________

Shield of ______________________________

Sword of ______________________________

The schemes of the devil are real, but our truest reality doesn't lay in the p ots of the evil one, but in the One who empowers us to live in His Immeasurably More. One of our points of confidence in Christ is found in the pieces of His heart that He gives us in order to stand firm in the face of attacks mounted on our desire to live in God's abundance. Each piece is grounded in the character of Jesus and represents our greatest hope, deepest joy, and securest confidence.

Truth is the foundation of God's Immeasurably More. When we dwell in Him, we live in truth. It lights our way, defines our path, and enables us to dwell securely in His presence. We can be confident in what God tells us.

Planting ourselves in the truth of Jesus ignites a transformation within us. We live in His truth, and His truth changes our nature. Integrity and honesty become central to our character. The wisdom of His truth helps us navigate through the fog of misdirection and illusion that surrounds It'll Do Lane. We move through our days with greater confidence as we take more of His truth into our hearts.

Are you growing in truth? How do we fill our lives with more of His truth?

Righteousness is the cornerstone of our confidence. God is always right. He never makes a mistake, has a misplaced motive, makes a wrong turn, or misjudges the moment. He always moves at the right time, in the right way, in the right direction for the right reasons.

When we put on His righteousness, He helps us not only be right, but do right. Looking more and more like Jesus increasingly involves making the right decisions at the right time from a heart that seeks His right. The more of His righteousness that we put on, the more Immeasurably More is ours.

Are you growing in righteousness? How do we increasingly put on more of His righteousness?

Peace pushes back the limits that confine our souls. God is peace. He gives it as a gift. It is what results from His sacrificial love. It creates possibilities where before there was only darkness, anxiety, and restlessness. When we live in His peace, He heals our souls and makes us whole.

Taking up His peace steadies us. It gives us balance and the ability to stand firm in a shaky world. His peace not only gives us poise, it transforms us into peacemakers. His light shines through the peace we carry with us, offering hope, renewal, and an invitation to rest at the cross.

Are you growing in peace? How do we stand in a deeper measure of His peace?

Faith is the response of a heart that opens its eyes to the presence of God. Faith opens our hearts to His movement, and is the fuel that propels us into His Immeasurably More. The longer we walk with God, the more of His faithfulness we experience, and the stronger our faith grows. The stronger our faith grows, the more our eyes and hearts are open to the way He surrounds us, moves in us, and speaks to us. Each step into deeper faith cements our hearts in the limitless possibilities of His Immeasurably More.

Immeasurably More

Are you growing in faith? How do we encourage our faith to be become stronger?

Salvation is the work of God on our behalves. His love moved when we were mired in sin. His grace cut a path through our guilt and shame in order to offer us a place by His side. Satan will constantly pick at the confidence we can have in the salvation God provides for us. Learning to live with surety within the salvation Christ purchased for us on the cross allows us to shut out the lies of It'll Do Lane. Understanding all He saved us from and calls us to gives us the confidence to embrace holiness and walk away from ungodliness.

Are you increasingly dependent on His grace? How do we walk deeper into the holiness to which He calls us?

The Word of God is the anthem of our hearts. Jesus is the Word of God. He is the full revelation of God to man, and He is ours. He dwells within us, taking up residence and transforming our hearts according to His good purpose.

The Word of God empowers us to hear the voice of God. It helps us see His hand, understand His will, and move in His love.

His Word reveals His standard. It calls us to surrender, and blesses us with an ever-expanding picture of who God is and how He longs to walk with us.

Are you growing in the Word of God? How do we let the Word of God penetrate our lives in an ever deeper way?

The pieces of His heart that Jesus gives us are the tools we need to withstand the attacks that spin from the devil's schemes. They will help us stand firm, keep our balance, maintain our focus, and stay connected to God. But don't miss the beauty of the picture. When we put on the armor of God, we are putting on the nature of Jesus. This is the transformation that is at the heart of God's Immeasurably More. When we put on the whole armor of God, we are living in God's Immeasurably More. We are covered in it, drenched in it, sheltered by it, and wrapped within it. Everything He wants for you is available to you right now. Put it on. It really is for you.

It'll Do Lane

Every day feels like a fight. It takes everything I have to get back up, but then the wind just gets knocked out of me again. I am not sure that it is even worth fighting any more. I will just do the best I can and hope it is enough.

Immeasurably More

God equips me for the battle that rages around me. I have a big enemy, but I have a bigger God. He covers me with Himself, calling me to stand in His presence and power. When I do, I stand in the midst of everything His Immeasurably More has for me.

Choosing a Home For Your Heart

The admonition in Ephesians 6:13 is to put on the *whole* armor of God. Walk back through the characteristics of Christ outlined in Ephesians 6:14-17. It tends to be easier for us to put on some of these characteristics than others. Which pieces of Christ's nature do you wear well? Which pieces of His heart do you need to more fully invest in?

Day 3

As we walk in God's Immeasurably More, God clothes us with Christ. He covers us in an armor that shines with His righteousness. We wear shoes that radiate with His peace, while faith and salvation plant our souls in His presence and power. The Word of God fills us with truth, direction, holiness, and wisdom. In clothing us with His heart, He is doing more than protecting us. He is ushering us into the depths of His Immeasurably More. It is when we are covered with Him that we experience all the richness, life, and abundance which defines what it means to be His. But there is one more thing God gives us that anchors our hearts in the fullness of His Immeasurably More.

Read Ephesians 6:18-20.

What are we to do at all times in the Spirit?

Immeasurably More

What encouragement does Paul give us with regard to prayer?

What specific prayer requests does Paul ask for himself?

There is one activity that will anchor us deeply in God's Immeasurably More – prayer. Prayer is the lifeline of a heart tied to the heart of God. It is the vehicle by which we pour out our hearts and open our lives to His transformation. In prayer, we interact with our God. He opens His presence, His heart, His grace, His power, His provision, and His faithfulness and invites us in. There we release all of our concerns, realign our priorities as we praise, gain new eyes through gratitude, and receive fresh grace to cover our sins.

In prayer, God pours Himself into us. He moves in our hearts to lift burdens, instill peace, ignite joy, and draw us closer to Himself. Prayer lifts our eyes, expands our vision, and pulls back the limits on what is possible.

Prayer is absolutely essential to a heart that longs to live in God's Immeasurably More. It is here that we invest ourselves in His presence. It is here that we lay our hearts in His hands, asking Him to unleash His power within us. It is here that we walk away from the settling that pulls at our souls and learn to fly in the spaciousness of His grace.

How invested are you in prayer?

The answer to that question, perhaps more than any other, is the best gauge to how deeply you are walking in His Immeasurably More. Prayer is certainly not the only component necessary to living in His abundance, but there is no one who lives in His Immeasurably More without it.

Let's walk with Jesus as He stretches the boundaries of how we see prayer.

Read John 14:13-14. What promise does Jesus make to you about the power of prayer?

Jesus makes us an extraordinary, amazing promise about prayer. If you ask me *anything* in my name, I will do it. It is a stunning assurance. Yet, for some reason it makes us nervous. We spend a lot of time explaining what *anything* isn't. Anything isn't a million dollars. It isn't the answer to our every desire. It *is* the entirety of His Immeasurably More. God's abundance is His will. Your transformation is His deepest longing. When you ask for His Immeasurably More to take hold of your life, He promises you that He will do it. Anything it takes, any measure needed, any power required, any grace necessary – anything to fill your life with the reality of His Immeasurably More. All you have to do is come with a surrendered heart and ask.

Read Matthew 17:20. What does Jesus promise we will be able to do with faith like a mustard seed?

Now Jesus stretches the boundaries a little farther. He gives us a specific picture of what is possible when we let faith plant us into His Immeasurably More. Mountains will move. What seems like the largest, most unmovable, most solid, and massive things in our eyes will move from here to there. When you throw a small seed at a mountain in the physical world, nothing happens. When you stand in the spiritual realm of God's Immeasurably More, a small seed is more than enough to knock a mountain off its foundations. Not because the seed is strong, but because the physics of power change when God holds the seed. We put the seed in His hand, and He moves the mountain.

What kind of mountains move? What are the mountains in your life? Sin, guilt, and shame make up a towering range in our vision. Ask, and they're gone. How about mountains of fear, doubt, and worry? Say to the mountain move, and it will move. Nagging anxiety, struggles with self-worth, and habits that hold us back? Throw a seed and stand back. *Nothing* will be impossible for you.

Anything and *nothing* are big words, but they are the words that mark the boundaries of the possibilities of prayer.

Read Ephesians 3:20-21. What promise does God make about His ability to work in us?

Now we enter the limitless possibilities of God's Immeasurably More. First, Jesus tells us that anything we ask is possible. Next, He promises that nothing will be impossible. Now, He stretches out His hands and offers us the full vista of His abundance. He is able to do *immeasurably more* than we can ask or imagine. Our prayers don't define the limits of His power. Our imaginations are not the stopping point for His dreams. He is able to go far beyond what our minds can envision in order for His vision to take full shape in our lives.

God is willing to give you far more than you can ask or imagine. He is able to unleash His power, ignite His joy, unfold His peace, and unharness His grace in your heart. He longs for you to ask, to imagine the possibilities and be willing to stand back and watch Him do far more abundantly than all we can think or dream. Pray and let Him open your eyes and your heart to His Immeasurably More.

In what way are you willing to let God stretch the boundaries of your prayers?

Day 4

Ephesians is a letter that invites us into God's Immeasurably More. Too often our hearts settle for so much less than the best God wants to give us. We come to It'll Do Lane, decide this is good enough, and build our lives on just getting by. Sometimes it is the world's lies that make us buy a place in the It'll Do neighborhood. Other times, circumstances rock our world and in the struggle to find answers, we pick It'll Do Lane because it seems like the safest of our options. But most of the time, we just slip into It'll Do. It isn't a conscious choice, a radical rebellion, or a definite decision. Just somewhere along the way, comfort and familiarity invite us to make a home where our hearts were really never supposed to rest. We wake up one day, realizing that the years have passed us by and life seems a little empty, our hearts are a little hard, and our hope seems a little dry. But what else is there? Maybe this will have to do.

Enter Jesus. Since before Adam and Eve settled for fruit rather than His favor, God has been making a plan to give you Immeasurably More. It breaks His heart to see you settle. It'll Do Lane was never supposed to be the address of your soul. His plan centered on sending His Immeasurably More to earth so that we could have a living, breathing picture of what it means to live in God's abundance. In a move beyond what we could have asked or dreamed about, Jesus hung on a cross and died, taking the sin of the world on His back. With power that defies imagination, He rose from the grave sending a tidal wave of grace coursing through the hearts of men.

It is into this Immeasurably More that God calls you to live. He longs to immerse you in His immeasurable love. He stands as Father ready to embrace you as His children. His immeasurable power, the same power that raised Jesus from the dead, is waiting to be unleashed in your life. His great delight would be to fill your soul with the immeasurable riches of His grace. Immeasurable peace is waiting to quiet your spirit. He has an immeasurable purpose for you. No more investing our hearts in things too small for our dreams. Immeasurable faith opens the door for all of God's Immeasurably More to fill our lives. And that is just the beginning. We start with what we can see and think about and then move into more than we can ask or imagine.

Which part of God's Immeasurably More most deeply calls to your heart today? Why?

God does more than just offer us the possibility of Immeasurably More. He lays out the process by which we can move out of It'll Do Lane and into the rich abundance of His presence. He calls us to walk with Him. Abraham has helped us learn how to do that as he takes the steps of faith necessary to walk as God's friend.

Read Hebrews 11:8-16.

What did faith compel Abraham to do?

To what was Abraham looking forward?

How did Sarah's faith release God's promises in her life?

How does verse 13 describe those who walk in this kind of faith?

What is their desire?

What is God prepared to do for those who walk with Him in faith?

Walk Called. Listen for the voice of God. Respond to the invitation He offers. Be willing to leave what is comfortable, close, and familiar in order to embrace the promises He wants to pour into your life.

Walk Changed. Transformation is at the heart of God's greatest desire for you. He wants to shape you into the image of His beloved Son. The purpose He is building in your life is one of His own design. It is built on the foundation of Jesus and rises as a testimony to His grace and faithfulness.

Walk Closely. God wants to walk in our most intimate moments. He wants to draw us ever closer to His heart and help us experience the tenderness of His mercy. Walking closely by His side allows the full power of His promises to touch who we are and stretch into the future.

Walk Committed. Walking with God requires obedience, surrender, submission, and sacrifice. It demands a commitment of our entire being – heart, soul, mind, and strength. The world will pull at us, trying to get us to compromise pieces of our commitment in order to lure us back to It'll Do Lane. God uses the things we hand to Him through surrender and obedience to open up even more of His Immeasurably More in our lives.

Walk Confidently. When we embrace the Immeasurably More life God offers us, we understand that this world is not our home. We are strangers and exiles as we look forward to a better country. Our confidence flows from Who we walk with, and the knowledge that the Immeasurably More we experience here is just a taste of the abundance to come.

To which aspect of walking with God do you need to more fully give yourself?

God calls you into the Immeasurably More life. It is something that you can experience right now, right here, right where you are. But here is the "more than we can ask or imagine" picture that takes our breath away. All the richness, abundance, joy, peace, love, power, and grace that is ours today is merely a sample of the Immeasurably More to come. Heaven is an eternity of exploring God's Immeasurably More.

This is what God wants for you. It is what He was willing to die to give you. The decision about whether to live in it or not is up to you. It'll Do Lane or God's Immeasurably More? The choice is yours.

I'll admit, sometimes life on It'll Do Lane seems a little hollow. But this is home. I have lived here a long time. Stepping out of the known into the unknown is just too scary and means I have to let go of being in control. Maybe tomorrow, but for today, it'll do.

God's Immeasurably More offers me the adventurous journey my soul craves. I choose to hold tightly to His hand, walk closely by His side, and take a step of faith toward the promise He will build in my life. By faith I declare that He really is able to do Immeasurably More in my life than I can ask or imagine.

Choosing a Home For Your Heart

Who do you know that lives in God's Immeasurably More? If you can, talk to them about your decision to leave It'll Do Lane and make your home in God's Immeasurably More. Ask them to share a piece of wisdom that will help you on your journey. Ask God to push back the boundaries of your *anything* and *nothing*. Pray for His Immeasurably More to take shape in your life and surrender to the possibility that He really is able to do more than you can ask or imagine.

Bibliography

Conybeare, W.J., and J.S. Howson. *The Life and Epistles of Saint Paul.* Hartford, CT: The S.S. Scranton Company, 1914. Print.

"Covet." *Dictionary.com Unabridged.* Random House, Inc. Web. 18 Apr. 2011.

The ESV Study Bible, English Standard Version. Wheaton, IL: Crossway Bibles, 2008. Print. Eng. Standard Vers.

The NET Bible, New English Translation. Richardson, TX: Biblical Studies Press, L.L.C., 1996. Print.

NIV Archaeological Study Bible. Grand Rapids, MI: Zondervan. 2005. Print.

The NIV Study Bible, 10th Anniversary Edition. Grand Rapids: Zondervan Publishing House, 1995. Print. New International Vers.

Peterson, Eugene. *The Message: The Bible in Contemporary Language.* Colorado Springs, CO: NavPress, 2002. Print.

Harper, Douglas. "Poem." *Online Etymology Dictionary.* 2010.Web. 09 Apr. 2011

Strong, J. *The exhaustive concordance of the Bible: Showing every word of the text of the common English version of the canonical books, and every occurence of each word in regular order.* Electronic ed. Ontario: Woodside Bible Fellowship, 1996.

Take Time For Yourself and Retreat Into The Heart of God
Relax, Read, and Reflect as Casandra Martin shows us the way into a deeper relationship with the Father.
Women Opening the Word
ABCs of a Godly Heart - 978-0-89098-300-3
Echoing His Heartbeat: the Life of David - 978-0-89098-301-0
Fragrance of Fatih: Discovering the Aroma of Christ in the Beatitudes - 0-89098-297-X
God Pass By Me: Study of the Names of God - 0-89098-257-0
Immeasurably More - 0-89098-303-4
A Light in the Darkness: Elijah and Elisha - 0-89098-295-3
Our Father in Heaven...Teach Us to Pray - 0-89098-298-8
Paul, By the Grace of God - 0-89098-296-1
Set Free - 978-0-89098-302-7
The Shadow of the Cross - 0-89098-262-7
That You May Believe: the Gospel of John - 0-89098-299-6
Tell Me the Story...
In this series for both men and women, Casandra and co-author Bill Rasco explore your favorite stories of faith from a fresh perspective.
The Armor of God - 978-0-89098-339-3
Meeting Jesus - 0-89098-338-0

Look Like Jesus
Make The Jesus Resolution

by Casandra Martin

Accept the invitation, found in this collection of devotional thoughts, for the amazing transformation that occurs when we strive to look like Jesus in each moment of every day. Whether you are doing laundry, washing dishes, or paying bills, you can learn to see God in every place and in every simple task. When God touches the ordinary with His presence, nothing is ever the same.

Make The Jesus Resolution today!

$12.99

978-0-89098-344-7